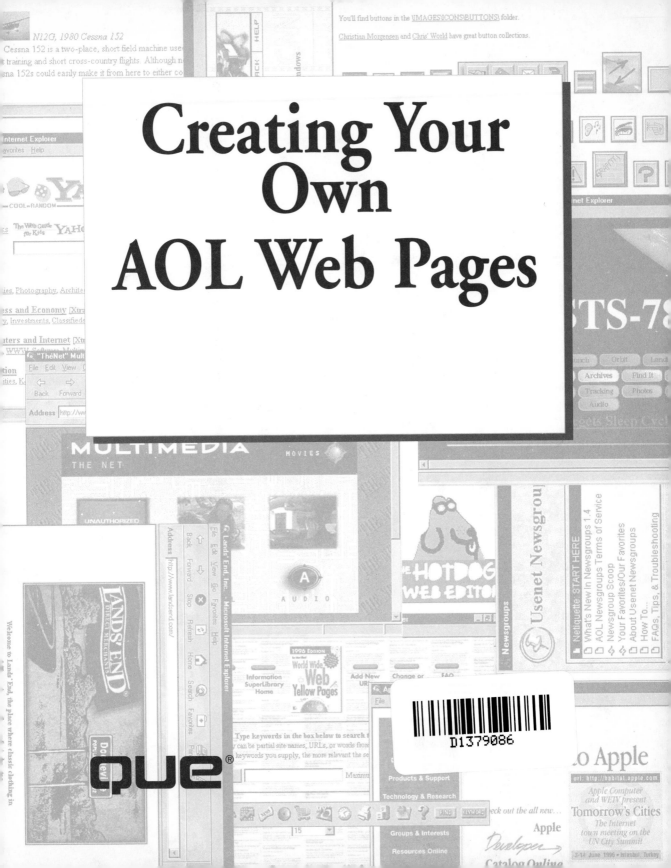

Creating Your Own Own AOL Web Pages

que®

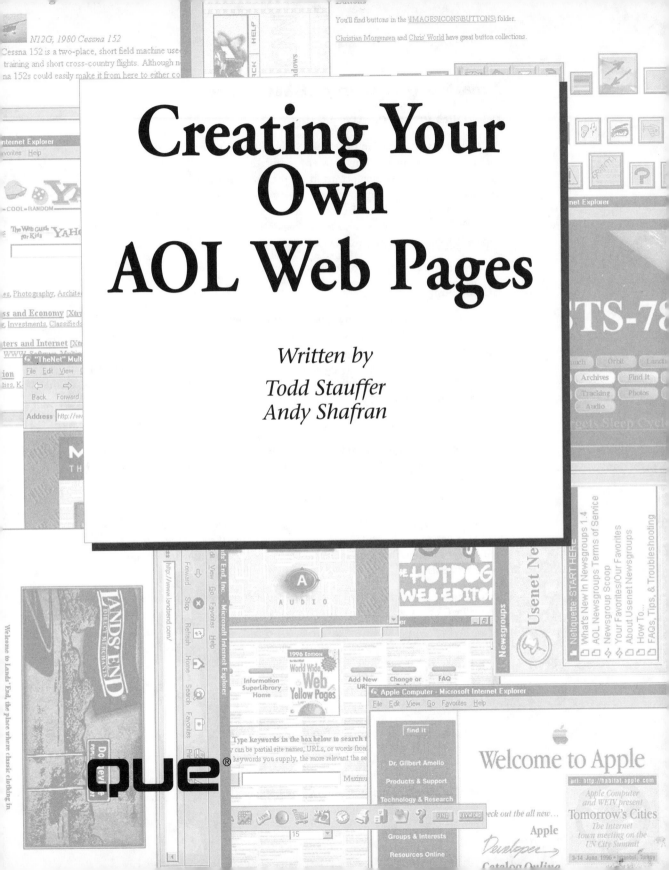

Creating Your Own
AOL Web Pages

Written by

Todd Stauffer
Andy Shafran

que®

Creating Your Own AOL Web Pages

Library of Congress Catalog No.: 96-69606

ISBN: 0-7897-0901-5

98 97 96   6 5 4 3 2 1

Interpretation of the printing code: the rightmost double-digit number is the year of the book's printing; the rightmost single-digit number, the number of the book's printing. For example, a printing code of 96-1 shows that the first printing of the book occurred in 1996.

Screen reproductions in this book were created using Capture from Mainstay, Camarillo, CA.

Composed in *Stone Serif* and *MCPdigital* by Que Corporation

Credits

To Kathy, who never seems to get enough credit. How's this? Thanks for everything.

About the Author

Todd Stauffer has been writing nonstop about computers since his graduation from Texas A&M University, where he studied English, Management Information Systems, and entirely too much golf. Since that time, he has worked as an advertising writer, freelance magazine writer, and magazine editor—all in the computer industry.

Todd is currently the Internet-issues columnist for *Peak Computing Magazine* and host of the weekly Peak Computing Hour Radio Show in Colorado. He has written a number of other books published by Que including *Using Your Mac, Using the Internet with Your Mac, Easy AOL, Special Edition Using Netscape, Special Edition Using the Internet with Your Mac*, and *HTML by Example*.

He does other, non-computer-related things, too—just in case you were concerned.

Acknowledgments

This book is based in no small part on the work of Andy Shafran, author of the original Creating series book, *Creating Your Own Netscape Pages*. You'll see my name (Todd) and Internet addresses throughout the text, but a good bit of the book remains Andy's work. I'd like to thank him for letting me work with him.

The rest of the book owes no small debt to Jim Minatel, Mark Cierzniak, Maureen Schneeberger, and Bill Bruns. We're almost getting good at this, aren't we? Thanks to them and the Que production staff for putting this project together.

Personally I'd like to thank Chris Stauffer (my dad) for helping me continue the transition to Colorado Springs and this new life as a freelance writer. I'd also like to thank Laura Austin-Eurich and Dean Jacobus at *Peak Computing Magazine* for their understanding during these projects (and the regular checks in my mailbox). I'll do my best to get back ahead of schedule on the column.

We'd Like to Hear from You!

As part of our continuing effort to produce books of the highest possible quality, Que would like to hear your comments. To stay competitive, we *really* want you, as a computer book reader and user, to let us know what you like or dislike most about this book or other Que products.

You can mail comments, ideas, or suggestions for improving future editions to the address below, or send us a fax at (317) 581-4663. Our staff and authors are available for questions and comments through our Internet site at **http://www.mcp.com/que**, and Macmillan Computer Publishing also has a forum on CompuServe (type **GO QUEBOOKS** at any prompt).

In addition to exploring our forum, please feel free to contact me personally to discuss your opinions of this book: I'm **mcierzniak@que.mcp.com** on the Internet, and **76245,476** on CompuServe.

Thanks in advance—your comments will help us to continue publishing the best books available on computer topics in today's market.

Mark Cierzniak
Product Development Specialist
Que Corporation
201 W. 103rd Street
Indianapolis, Indiana 46290
USA

Contents at a Glance

Contents

3 Building a Simple Web Page with AOL Online Tools 51

II Creating a Basic Web Page 67

4 The Web Page Basics 69

9 Clickable Image Maps and Beyond   **165**

10 Making Your Web Page Multimedia   **179**

IV Adding the Final Touches to Your AOL Web Pages   **191**

11 Important Design Considerations   **193**

12 Publicizing Your Web Page 209

Appendixes 225

A AOL Online Web Resources 227

B Home Page Final Checklist 231

Introduction

Did you know that having an America Online account automatically entitles you to free space on AOL's computers for your very own World Wide Web home page? Forget about worrying over a special Internet account, buying special tools, or taking a Web publishing class. You don't even need a "direct" connection to the Internet.

With an AOL membership and this book, you'll be creating a home page on the Web in a matter of minutes.

If you're anything like me, you're comfortable with the AOL interface, and you enjoy using America Online for a lot of the online work you need to get done. And now you've got something else to do with your AOL account—create a presence for yourself or your business on the Web.

It's easy to do and you'll have your page up in no time. (Notice that this isn't exactly a huge book!) In fact, with a little practice, you'll have a new job skill. Are you ready to put a Web page address on your business card? Do you have a hobby you'd like to share with the world? Are you job hunting and want to show off your computer saavy? Let's go!

What You'll Learn in This Book

This book is geared toward teaching you what you need to know about home page publishing with the AOL service. I'll take you step-by-step through the entire process, from concept to finished product.

Specifically, you'll learn how to do the following:

- Plan your home page and learn to deal with AOL's tools
- Effectively use an HTML editor
- Create a basic home page
- Organize information with lists and tables
- Link your home page to others throughout the world
- Incorporate other Internet resources, such as FTP and Gopher, with your home page

- Embed pictures, audio clips, and video clips into your home page
- Use proper home page design techniques
- Maintain your home page to keep it current and interesting
- Expand your home page into a sophisticated Web site
- Attract visitors from around the world to your pages

Practical Explanations, not Concepts

I'm going to take you through the real life issues that you face while creating your home page. It's true—you could probably spend enough time worrying about Web technology and programming to fulfill the requirements for a master's degree. But you don't have to. A combination of America Online's tools and the tools included with the book are all you need to make a Web page work for you.

I'm not going to waste much of your time writing about the intricacies of HTML, arguments over Internet bandwidth, or other issues that probably don't interest you. Instead, you'll find a step-by-step guide to help you accomplish all your home page goals.

Introduction to HTML Tools, not HTML Tutorial

Home pages are written in HyperText Markup Language (HTML). While HTML is not overly difficult, some concepts can be hard to understand and work with.

That's why I've chosen to include a special HTML editor with this book. Using this editor, you won't have to learn all the details of HTML programming. Instead, you can use the HTML editor to take care of the programming for you. You don't need to be an HTML expert to have a great-looking home page. And it's more important to concentrate on a well-designed, informative page anyway.

Who Should Use This Book?

Anyone who has experienced the World Wide Web, and wants to create his or her own unique home page, will be interested in this book. In general, the beginner- and average-level World Wide Web surfer and Internet user will find this book a suitable and complete tool for creating home pages.

We'll talk very specifically about some of the issues that AOL user's will face when you're ready to create a home page. If you don't have an active account, I'd recommend signing up. You can even get away with paying the minimum membership for AOL and be able to put up a Web page.

I have made a couple of assumptions about you, the reader, while writing this book:

- **You've seen the Web**—It's important that you understand what the World Wide Web is, and have a rudimentary understanding of how it works (I'll go over this in more detail in the first chapter). You should know the difference between Netscape (a WWW browser) and Microsoft Excel (not a browser). You don't have to be an Internet guru, but passing familiarity helps.

- **You have an active AOL account**—There are few things easier in the computing world than getting your hands on an America Online disk. Most newsstands offer magazines that bundle the software every month. AOL gives you some special tools, help, and up to 10 MB of free space for your Web pages. If you don't have an AOL account, call 1-800-827-6364 to order their client software.

- **You've upgraded to at least AOL version 3.0**—The latest versions of the America Online service include the Microsoft Internet Explorer Web browser. That's the browser we'll use and talk about a lot throughout this book. If you haven't upgraded, I'd recommend it. Most of the tools and procedures we'll discuss will still work for you, but your results might vary from the majority of the figures in this book.

How This Book Helps You Create Your Home Page

The tasks in *Creating Your Own AOL Web Pages* are organized to walk you through the process of creating a very good home page. The book starts with planning your home page and continues through the development cycle until your initial page is complete. Finally, you announce your home page to the Web world.

Each chapter is broken down into managable chunks of information that make it easy to digest the process of creating a home page. There's no fluff and not much technical jargon. Think of each chapter as a new lesson, with tips on making the best Web pages you possibly can.

Here is a brief summary of what you'll find in this book and how it is organized.

Part I—Planning Your Web Page

This part includes the first three chapters of the book. Chapter 1, "A Web Crawler's Beginning," gives a basic introduction to the World Wide Web and contains important information detailing how the Web works. You'll also learn what a home page is.

In Chapter 2, "Starting to Weave Your Own Web," I discuss how to go about planning and organizing your home page as well as show you several different example home pages that already exist on the WWW. You'll be introduced to HotDog, the HTML editor used throughout the book. You'll also learn how to upload your pages to AOL to make them publically available on the Web.

Chapter 3, "Building a Simple Web Page with AOL Online Tools," covers the special Personal Publisher tools on America Online. This service of AOL allows you to create a very simple Personal Publisher Home page, complete with links to other Web pages, graphics, and multimedia files. It's not as flexible as creating pages yourself, but you'll be up on the Web in a matter of minutes.

Part II—Creating a Basic Web Page

Read through this part to get up to speed on the basics of creating a home page. Chapter 4, "The Web Page Basics," overviews how to add text and text formatting features to your home page while keeping the information easy to read. In addition, you'll also learn how to break up blocks of text and what elements of HTML every Web page should have.

Continue on with Chapter 5, "Adding Lists and Tables to Your Web Page," for an explanation of how to use and include tables and lists on your home page. This chapter not only explains how to use lists and tables effectively, but also helps you decide when you want to use them as well.

Chapter 6, "Spicing Up Your Web Pages with Graphics," helps you add some personality to your home page. Text and tables are nice-looking, but most attractive home pages include images and links to other sites on the WWW. Chapter 6 teaches you how to integrate graphics and pictures on your home page. You'll learn how to use some of the images from the included CD-ROM or pictures of your own as important parts of your page. There's even a special service from AOL that helps you turn snapshots into electronic graphics files.

In Chapter 7, "Linking Web Pages Together," I show you how to add and organize hypertext links to your home page. You'll learn how to link your document to any other spot on the Web. In addition, you'll see how to use graphics as hotlinks and how to sort and organize links without overwhelming the folks who visit your page.

Part III—Spicing Up Your Web Page

In Chapter 8, "Cool Ways to Customize Your Web Page," I'll demonstrate advanced ways to customize your home page. You'll learn how to incorporate additional World Wide Web and Netscape features by splitting your home page into several different pages, tracking the number of visitors who stop by and browse, and using other Internet resources (such as FTP and UseNet) as part of your page.

Chapter 9, "Clickable Image Maps and Beyond," discusses the exciting new client-side image map technology. With tools on the CD-ROM, you can quickly create clickable image interfaces for your Web page—just like the interfaces that the big-time companies use on their Web sites.

In Chapter 10, "Making Your Web Page Multimedia," we'll discuss creating and adding special multimedia elements to your Web page.

Part IV—Adding the Final Touches to Your AOL Web Pages

Before your home page is completed, you should read through Part IV and learn how to clean up and publicize your home page on the Internet. Read Chapter 11, "Important Design Considerations," to learn several design issues regarding home page publishing. You'll learn design tips that will make your page(s) exciting to look at and easy to maintain in the future. We'll also talk about some of the special considerations that AOL users need to make.

In Chapter 12, "Publicizing Your Web Page," I'll teach you how to let other WWW users know that your home page exists—what good is a home page that no one ever visits? You'll learn the proper channels of publicity, and where to announce to the Internet that you're ready for them to stop by and see the fruits of your labor.

Appendixes

Several appendixes are provided for your benefit. Use them as references for the book and while you are creating your home page.

Appendix A, "AOL Online Web Resources," tells you about the number of different areas and discussion groups that America Online offers to help you learn about and work with the Web.

Appendix B, "Home Page Final Checklist," contains a simple checklist to make sure you've caught most of the common mistakes new home page creators make. I've also summarized some of the common tips and tricks.

Appendix C, "References Used in This Book," lists just what it says. On the Web, it's important to be able to cross-reference the information you find, and this book about the Web should be no exception. As you become more adept at Web page creation, there are a number of cool sites you'll want to visit for more information.

Appendix D, "What's on the CD-ROM?," lists the files and an explanation of what is included on the CD-ROM found in the back of this book.

Programs Used in This Book

This book is meant to be used as a tutorial, taking you through the process of using your computer to create your own home page. There are several computer programs that can help in this process, and in this book I highlight three of them—Internet Explorer, the AOL client software, and HotDog. These three tools and this book will guide you through any of the rough waters in the home page creation process.

Internet Explorer

Internet Explorer is Microsoft's fast-flying competitor for dominance on the Web. Internet Explorer and Netscape Navigator dominate the Web browsing world, and for good reason.

Netscape has pioneered the user-driven improvement of HTML and the Web. Internet Explorer supports nearly all of Netscape's technology and special commands—and it even adds a few of its own. More importantly, though, Internet Explorer is included as the default Web browser for AOL members—an estimated 6 million (and growing) potential visitors to our home pages.

America Online

You'll need the America Online software to access the service, upload your Web pages, and use Internet Explorer via the AOL service. AOL also offers some exceptional areas on the service itself that you can visit to learn more about HTML, the Web, and some of the tools available for you.

There's a lot to learn on AOL, and a lot of folks are getting together to chat about creating Web pages for AOL. Not to mention that using the AOL software is the only way you can access your free Web space!

HotDog

HotDog is a top-notch HTML editor that takes the bite out of HTML programming and publishing. Using HotDog, you don't have to be familiar with all the intricacies of HTML codes, tags, and special characters. Instead, HotDog takes care of many of these complications.

HotDog, in my personal opinion, is the best of the available HTML editors for Windows and Windows 95. A shareware version is included on the CD-ROM in the back of this book, and I'll show you how install it in Chapter 2. The rest of the book focuses on using HotDog to create your Web page and simplifying this process.

Conventions Used in This Book

As you're reading through the book, I use several different conventions that highlight specific types of information. Most of the following conventions are designed to make creating AOL Web pages easier, so please take note:

- All HTML codes and tags appear in ALL MONOSPACE CAPS. (Browsers actually don't care whether your HTML tags are in full caps.)

- All URLs are displayed in **boldface**. You can type them directly into your browser and go directly to the site referred to.

- *Italic type* is used to introduce new terms.

- Text that you are asked to type appears in **boldface**.

- Text that appears on-screen is indicated by a `special computer font`.

- In this book, some menu and dialog box options have underlined characters, such as <u>F</u>ile. This indicates that it is a mnemonic key. To choose the option using the mnemonic key, press the Alt key and then press the indicated mnemonic key (in this example, Alt+F).

You can find referenced files, graphics, and templates on the CD-ROM found in the back of this book. This icon indicates text that describes the files on the CD-ROM.

On the CD

Tip

Tips offer extra advice on creating your Web page. I included personal anecdotal experiences, as well as specific design techniques in these extra bits of information.

Note

Notes provide special comments, important information, and other ways of getting something done. Sometimes these are just reminders, but often they offer another way to look at a particular issue.

Caution

Actions that could make permanent changes or potentially cause problems in the future are highlighted as Cautions. You'll want to take note of the Caution sections because they could warn of an irreversible decision, or prevent damage to your home page.

The Other Reason to Buy This Book

In my career as a technical book author, I've found that this part of the introduction is generally the most highly praised among readers. You see, I believe it's important that you have my e-mail address.

Helping you is my job; it's why you paid me, and I'm happy to get any e-mail messages with comments, concerns, praise, or—most importantly—questions. You bought my book, and I was supposed to have written it well enough that you are able to get your Web page online without too much trouble.

If that isn't the case, send me a message. I'll respond as quickly as possible, and somehow we'll work it out. (I once spent an hour on the phone with a reader; I ended up sending her a disk through the mail to solve a problem.)

You can write me on AOL at the screen name **TStauffer**. From the Internet, that's **tstauffer@aol.com**. I also maintain my own Web site that takes advantage of AOL's free Web page space. You can find my site at **http://members.aol.com/tstauffer/** for updates, reader comments, and some information about me. Hopefully, my pages offer a good way for you to learn what's possible on the Web and with the AOL service. Feel free to use the Edit, View Source command in your browser to see how I've created my pages.

Once you have your page up and available on the Web, send me an e-mail and tell me about it. I'll add it to a listing for all *Creating Your Own AOL Web Pages* readers, and maybe, together, we can point some visitors toward your home page. (Use the format I outline in Chapter 12 for submitting pages to me for the reader listing.)

I'll see you on the Web! ❖

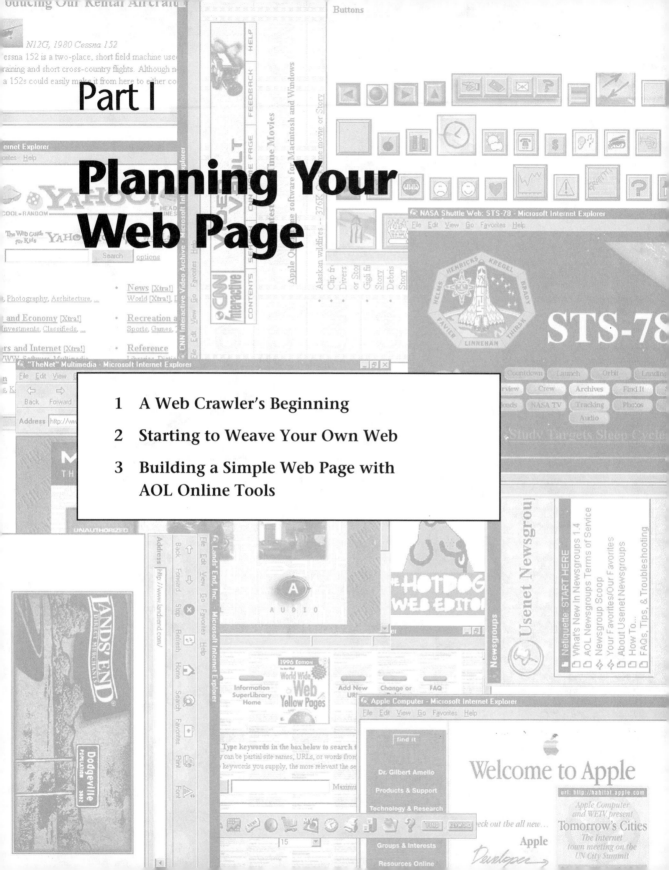

Part I

Planning Your Web Page

CHAPTER 1

A Web Crawler's Beginning

By the time you've picked up this book and decided to create your own Web pages, you will have easily spent several days, weeks, or even months "surfing" the Internet and exploring the World Wide Web. In this chapter, I introduce and explain the Web, and make sure you understand several concepts before you start creating your own Web page.

A new chain of stores is popping up around the nation. These stores carry video and sound equipment and a fully stocked inventory of albums, CDs, and software, as well as a complete bookstore. They are true "multimedia" stores—more like warehouses, actually. Now, let's take that same concept and make it available electronically. What do you have? The World Wide Web— sort of. Of course, the Web isn't owned by one central entity—you're free to open up your own "store" on the Web. And you can sell or distribute just about anything you want, using graphics, movies, text, sounds, and many other cool technologies.

What is the World Wide Web?

Simply put, the World Wide Web is a graphical way of retrieving information using the Internet. On the Web, you can find information relating to any topic imaginable, right from your home computer. With a graphical interface, you can browse through pages and pages of text, scan through tons of pictures, and even experience some audio and video clips. The WWW also integrates with other popular parts of the Internet such as Gopher and FTP, making it your one-stop shopping trip for exploring the Internet.

A textbook definition of the Web might be "a multimedia, hypertext environment using a markup language that supports multiple Internet protocols."

That's a good definition of the WWW if you completely understand what it means. Let me break down that sentence for you, just in case.

Multimedia

While most of the information found on the Internet is in straight text format, sometimes a picture is worth a thousand words (or more). One of the main features of the WWW is the ability to view images and text alike on the same screen. That makes using the Web graphical, fun, and exciting (see fig. 1.1).

Fig. 1.1
An example of multimedia at the home page for the movie "The Net" (**http:// www.spe. sony.com/ Pictures/ SonyMovies/ netmulti.html**).

Besides pictures and images, audio bites and video clips are also a cornerstone of the Web. Any site on the Web can integrate all four types of media into a single WWW page.

Movie studios regularly take advantage of the multimedia facets of the Web. On one screen you can read a movie review, see a picture of the movie poster, hear an actor recount his experience, and even see a preview of the movie at the same time.

Hypertext Links

The Web is a *hypertext* environment. Hypertext means that certain information that you see is "linked" to other pieces of information. For instance, when you use the Help feature in software such as Word or Excel, you'll find highlighted words that, by clicking them, take you to help for that word. Similarly, by clicking your mouse on a hypertext link on a Web page, you automatically bring up the linked information as a separate document.

These hypertext links are the basic building blocks of the Web. Every document is comprised of links that take you to other Web sites, pictures, sounds, files, and other related information.

On the Web, these different places and links are identified by *Uniform Resource Locators* (*URLs*). Every document and file on the Internet has its own unique URL that allows it be linked to other documents easily. You can think of these URLs as addresses. Each address has the following three basic elements:

> **Note**
>
> It will probably be easier to read this book if you think of URL as if it were pronounced like the name "Earl." Also, notice that URLs use the UNIX convention of forward slashes (/) as opposed to the back slashes of the DOS world.

- **URL Type**—The beginning of each URL identifies the type of link it is. For instance, **http://** indicates a Web link, **gopher://** indicates a Gopher link, **ftp://** indicates a link to an FTP site, and so on.

- **Server Address**—Following the URL type is the server address of the computer that holds the page. For instance, Microsoft's Web address is **www.microsoft.com**, so the URL for their hypertext Web site would be **http://www.microsoft.com/**.

> **Note**
>
> It's not terribly common, but it's possible for one server address to serve data for more than one type of URL. For instance, if Microsoft decided to make the server **www.microsoft.com** both an FTP and a Web server, you'd access the FTP server by simply changing the URL type, as in **ftp://www.microsoft.com/**. It's not likely to happen with larger companies, but some small companies or individuals will use one server address for all of their Internet links.

- **Directory or Document**—If a link is going to a particular document or directory, this would be attached to the end of the URL. For example, Microsoft has some shortcuts to the Internet in a document called ShortCuts.htm in the /Misc directory on its Web server. So if you wanted to access this document, the entire URL would be **http://www.microsoft.com/Misc/ShortCuts.htm**.

Let's say you were looking at a Web page of a local flying club, shown in figure 1.2. Since this is a fictitious home page designed for this chapter, it does not have an URL. From this screen, you can link to other pages that show you more information about the planes, the instructors, and rates. The links to other places are usually underlined or appear in a different color so they're easy to identify.

Fig. 1.2
Our fictitious flying club's "home" page is the start of our hypertext journey.

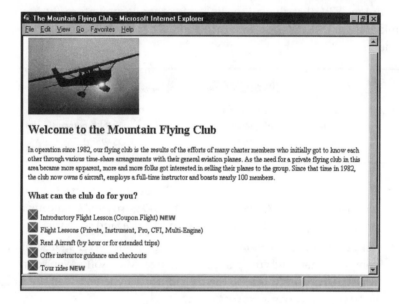

If you select the link to the planes (**Rent Aircraft** in fig. 1.2), you'll be brought to the "hanger" page, where you can look at the specifications and pictures of the planes in the flying club (see fig. 1.3). There are also additional links that bring you to other plane-related resources on the Web—perhaps the home page for the manufacturer of the plane, or photos taken by a flying magazine that can be found online. These links have nothing to do with the flying club, but are interesting to people who like planes. You might even end up following links to Air Force installations, the FAA, or maps of particularly pretty sites for flying over.

That's how the Web works. Related information is linked together in any way the Web author chooses. In this way, hypertext is incredibly flexible, allowing you to follow free-flowing paths to the information you need. In fact, some folks feel that hypertext works a little like the human brain—associating related information through a web of links.

HTML

The World Wide Web is based on a text markup language called *HyperText Markup Language* (*HTML*). HTML is a subset of an existing, more complicated language named SGML. Why a subset? HTML was designed specifically for the Web, SGML was not.

Fig. 1.3
Digging deeper into the flying club's Web information is easy—just click a hypertext link.

What is SGML?

The Standardized General Markup Language (SGML) is an agreed-to standard for document creation, remarkable in that it is both non-proprietary (publically available) and implicit in its formatting. This allows SGML to be useful for a number of different applications, from printing to paper to displaying online.

To understand SGML and its subset, HTML, consider a Microsoft Word .DOC format document. Since Microsoft's format is proprietary, it isn't used in any non-Microsoft programs. The format must be translated to be used in WordPerfect, for instance. At the same time, the Word file format is very useful for printing to paper, but not terribly useful for creating hypertext documents.

(continues)

(continued)

SGML allows for flexibility across both applications and platforms. This is achievable because SGML doesn't tell computers incredibly specific things about the way text should be displayed. Generally speaking, you'll rarely mark a particular word as bold, 24-point Times Roman in SGML or its subset, HTML. (You might do this in Microsoft Word, since it can be assumed that such a font exists on the user's particular computer.) Instead, you tell it that you want text to be emphasized or perhaps used as a heading.

So why not just use SGML, instead of HTML? Well, HTML is a specific definition of some of SGML's abilities, created exclusively for use on the World Wide Web. HTML is designed primarily for Web browsers, instead of for printing to paper or use with an online help program. HTML also happens to be readily understood by humans, which is a big plus. "Raw" SGML documents are designed to be interpreted by computer programs, so they can't easily be hand edited.

The important thing to remember is that HTML isn't really a programming language. A *markup* language uses tags that are inserted into textual documents that explain how information should be formatted on-screen. All HTML documents are purely text-based (which means you could easily load them into a text editor, like Windows Notepad, and read them without assistance). Web browsers, such as Internet Explorer or the older AOL browser, read the HTML documents and determine how to display that information on-screen. For example, the following line of HTML marked-up text would result in the entire line being boldface, with the word "my" in italics:

```
<B>This is <I>my</I> home page</B>
```

Tags determine which text should appear larger (as headlines), how paragraphs are formatted, where graphics should be placed, and how to link to other WWW pages. You'll learn all about the proper usage of tags as you read through this book.

Internet Protocols

There's a lot more to the Web than simply hyperlinking thousands of different documents together. The Web uses its own communications device, called the HTTP protocol, to send and receive pages across the Internet. *HTTP (HyperText Transfer Protocol)* is an Internet protocol that allows two computers to talk to each other in a specified format. However, HTTP is not the only Internet protocol supported by the WWW.

Using the Web and HTML, you can integrate the following Internet "services," or protocols, into your Web pages:

- **UseNet**—For access to Newsgroups (discussion groups) around the world
- **FTP**—Used for uploading and downloading files using *File Transfer Protocol*
- **Gopher**—A menu-based "low level" version of the Web which links different resources on the Internet
- **WAIS (Wide Area Information Service)**—Provides a way to search a variety of different databases
- **Telnet**—Allows you to directly connect to other computers on the Internet
- **E-mail**—For sending messages across the world electronically

The Web gives you convenient access to all of these different Internet services, together in one place.

How the Web Works

This is the only section where I am going to go into more technical detail about the underlying way the World Wide Web works. As you explore the Web and start creating your own Web pages, you'll find it useful to understand the different pieces that comprise the Web and how they all fit together.

Client/Server Based

The Web is a *client/server* application, which means that somewhere there exists a computer running Web server software and many different users (like you and me) who are clients, using Web browsers, accessing information from the Web server.

Web servers help send information back and forth to users across the world, they maintain connections with other Web servers, and they keep track of important usage statistics, such as the number of visitors to a specific Web page. Currently, there are nearly 50,000 Web servers on the Internet that are constantly talking to each other.

Perhaps you can think of it this way. Each Web server contains all of the protocols and information available on a particular site—where the documents are, whether there are executable programs that can be accessed, and more.

When you use your browser to access that Web site, the server jumps into action by providing the information that your browser is requesting.

To use a previous example, when you tell your browser to "go" to **http://www.microsoft.com/Misc/ShortCuts.htm**, Microsoft's Web server first interprets your request from the browser, finds the /Misc directory, locates the ShortCuts.htm document, and "serves" the contents of that document across the Internet to your browser. Finally, the browser takes that information and translates the code in the file into a viewable document.

Note

Since the Web is a distributed system with servers across the globe, there is no central Web server that controls the others. Thus, if a particular Web server becomes inactive, all of the other servers operate fine in its absence. If there was one central computer that ran into problems, millions of Web surfers would be out of luck.

Accessing the Web with AOL

Access to the Web usually requires a special Internet connection that is client/server based. *SLIP* (*Serial Line Internet Protocol*) and *PPP* (*Point-to-Point Protocol*) give Web users a "direct" connection to the Internet through an Internet service provider (ISP). The key advantage in this system is that you get to use whatever applications you want to access the various Internet services. Many different applications have been written for e-mail, UseNet newsgroups, and even browsing the Web—witness the popularity of Netscape, Internet Explorer, Mosaic, and others. With a "direct" connection like SLIP or PPP then, you can browse the Web, download e-mail, and read news all at once with programs you choose on your own.

AOL members, however, use a different system. Through your regular AOL account, you can dial up the AOL service, and then fire up Internet Explorer or the older AOL browser. You're essentially limited to the applications that AOL makes available, since your connection to the Internet isn't exactly a "direct" connection. Instead, the special AOL application software acts as a go-between for your computer and the Internet. As AOL's software becomes more sophisticated, it has begun to offer more choices. But, at least at the time of this writing, you are still pretty much limited to using only the AOL e-mail system, for instance, and the AOL UseNet newsreader (see fig. 1.4). With a direct connection, you could choose from a variety of applications.

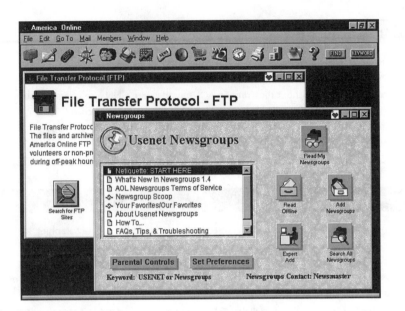

Fig. 1.4
AOL, in many
cases, requires you
to use its own
programs for
accessing the
Internet.

But things definitely aren't all bad. AOL has made great strides in allowing its
users to choose their own way to access the Web. Micrsoft's Internet Explorer
is the default browser for AOL users, and it's very capable. Netscape Navigator
is also a choice for AOL members, and using it to browse the Web is a very
complete solution. On top of that, both Internet Explorer and Netscape Navigator have built-in UseNet newsreaders and other features that make the AOL
Internet experience more flexible than ever before.

And there are some important advantages to AOL's Web access. Using AOL to
browse the Web lets you deal with both the special content on AOL in addition to the content that's available to regular Internet users. In fact, AOL
often integrates Web sites into the various areas on its service, which might
make those Web sites easier to find. Click one of AOL's links to the Web and
AOL's browser is automatically started up. Regular Web users have to jump
through some extra hoops to find good Web sites.

And don't forget the biggest advantage—free space for your Web site. You'll
need to have an active AOL account to put your pages in the free space provided on AOL's Web servers, and that's a huge part of what we're discussing
in this book!

For now, if you use the AOL service exclusively for Internet and Web access,
you should be just fine. Of course, any AOL user can also opt to use America
Online's GNN service (direct Internet access) or any of hundreds of other
Internet service providers (ISPs) around the world that offer Web access.

Note

The *Global Network Navigator* (*GNN*) is direct Internet service from America Online. GNN gives you access to the Web and other Internet services through its own connection software, without requiring an AOL membership. GNN also offers a "catalog" of the Web available for anyone's use at **http://www.gnn.com/**. The service's members get up to 20 MB of free Web space as part of their membership. Call 1-800-819-6112 for GNN customer service.

Caution

Since you will be using your AOL connection to transfer a lot of data (graphics, audio, and other resources take up a lot of room), you will want to also make sure you have a high-speed modem. A 14.4 modem is sufficient, but using a 28.8 will deliver better performance and is recommended. Another option is getting an ISDN card or adapter for your computer, along with an ISDN connection from your local phone company. This option isn't available everywhere, and you'll want to make sure that AOL offers a local number for ISDN access. But, if it does, it might be worth it when you get serious about your Web site. Realize, though, that ISDN service is always considerably more expensive; both the equipment and ISDN line will cost at least twice what a regular modem and phone line cost. (For more on AOL and ISDN, go to keyword **ISDN** on the service.)

History/Future of the Web

The Web has been around since early 1989, when a group of research scientists at CERN (The European Laboratory for Particle Physics in Switzerland) came up with the concept of how the Web would work. They released their work in 1991 and started generating interest in it. The scientists were significant in the setup of the W3 Consortium, the powers that dictate the next generation of HTML and the Web.

After being used sparingly for about a year, Mosaic—the first popular, graphical Web browser—was released and received rave reviews. Developed by the National Center for Supercomputing Applications (NCSA) at the University of Illinois, Urbana-Champaign, Mosaic was easy to use, available on the UNIX, PC, and Macintosh platforms, and distributed freely. Not long after, the original developer of Mosaic partnered with Silicon Graphics to create Netscape Navigator, today's reigning browser software. It is estimated that over 80 percent of all Web traffic worldwide comes from people using Netscape.

Since that time, both AOL and Microsoft have gotten heavily involved in creating browsers. AOL's first (and still popular) Web browser came from a licensed version of the Mosaic software, built specially to deal with the demands of the AOL service. Since that time, Microsoft and AOL have agreed to use the Microsoft Internet Explorer with future incarnations of the AOL service software. Internet Explorer is now Netscape's major competition, and does a good job of offering the "latest and greatest" for Web users.

Since Mosaic was introduced, the Web has become exponentially more popular every year. In less than four years, the Web has surpassed every other popular Internet application including FTP, e-mail, and Gopher, to be the world's heaviest-used piece of the Internet.

There are millions of Web pages to visit, each with its own unique content and identity.

Levels of HTML

When HTML, the underlying formatting language of the Web, was initially developed, it had limited functionality and text formatting characteristics. Since then, HTML has undergone a major revision, and the current standard is HTML 2.0.

Although HTML 2.0 offers quite a bit of flexibility to Web developers, it is only the beginning. Additional support for images, tables, and text formatting characteristics are in high demand. Web developers have long been asking for additional HTML support to enhance Web page graphic design and allow for more formatting control.

Fortunately, the next generation of HTML, version 3.2, has recently been agreed to by the W3 Consortium. Included in this next version are many new elements, added to give increased Web page flexibility.

Over the past year or so, while waiting for HTML 3.2, Netscape has announced its own enhancements to HTML, called Netscape HTML extensions. These extensions allow for increased text control and graphic support—almost everything that is included with HTML 3.2—only available to use now. Internet Explorer has followed suit by implementing nearly all of the Netscape commands, and even introducing some of its own.

Where possible, this book will teach you the HTML 3.2 standard commands—as long as I feel they've been widely implemented. For the first time in Web history, this is a standard that has been approved by nearly all of the major players in the Web market, including Netscape and Microsoft. So, we'll talk mostly about the standard commands, which should help you create pages that nearly everyone can see.

So, What's a Home Page?

Think of a large city. There are commercial buildings, industrial buildings, and residences. Every building has its own unique identity, from large skyscrapers to fast food restaurants. They all have their own atmosphere and flavor. When you buy your own house, you get the opportunity to decorate and landscape it however you like. You can keep your house prim and proper with all the shrubs trimmed, or let weeds overtake your lawn.

Creating your own home page is a similar concept. After all, it's your *virtual* "home." There are thousands of home pages out there for businesses, organizations, and individuals. On your page, you'll get to choose what type of information and/or graphics to make available, how it looks when people stop by for a visit, and how to keep it properly maintained.

There are no home page police who will stop by and make sure that everything is designed so that it's easy to use and the information on your home page is current. Your only restrictions are following the laws of your country and locality (most notably, copyright, pornography, and privacy laws). And it takes some effort to create an attractive and innovative home page that people will want to visit time and time again.

Read on to the next chapter to learn where and how to start building your own home page. You'll learn how to think through the home page process, how to sketch out and organize your page, and what tools will make it easier to construct your page. And I promise you'll have some fun in the process. ❖

CHAPTER 2

Starting to Weave Your Own Web

In the last chapter, I gave an overview of the World Wide Web, which included a brief explanation of a home page. Now you're ready to learn how to create your own personal home page and make it available for the millions of people on the Internet to check out.

Why Create a Home Page?

There are literally millions of Web pages out there right now for anyone on the Web to access. With that much information, no one will ever have time to see it all. One question you have to ask is, what could you possibly contribute? Why do you want to put a home page on the Web?

Home pages come in all different shapes and sizes. Some are merely personalized Internet vanity plates, while others offer unique information found nowhere else (such as the floating fish-cam page—a Web page that takes snapshots of an aquarium periodically throughout the day). Many people offer their services or sell products directly through their home pages.

Some people have Web pages just for fun; others just heard about the Web and thought a home page would be cool. The key then, is to decide what *your* reason for having a Web page is. With a specific goal in mind, you'll make better design choices.

And there really is no wrong answer. If you want to create a page for yourself, your family, or friends—just for fun—great! You've got free Web space on AOL and plenty of tools at your disposal. If you feel like it's important to have a site for your business, you're probably right about that, too. But you'll want to make sure you take extra care to design a site that makes your business look good.

> **Note**
>
> Personally, I think everyone should have their own Web page so they can create a unique environment that reflects their personality. My Web page reflects my interests and lets others with the same interests interact with me.
>
> My Web pages are not designed specifically to sell my services or promote my products, although you can definitely find that information there. I have two main goals: tell people about myself and my interests, and have a little fun discussing my books while adding new information for my readers.

Once you've decided why you want a home page, your next decision is what information should appear on it. As I've said, having an established home page goal will make it tremendously easier for you to design and create your pages on the Web.

Personal Pages

The vast majority of Web pages out there are personal home pages, created by individuals just like you and me. Ironically, personal pages are the pages you're least likely to visit because of the following:

- There are so many of them and they aren't indexed by category.
- They aren't as cool as some of the impressive, commercial sites.

However, personal home pages offer you your own customized place on the WWW and allow you to share information with your friends, family, and other Internet denizens. Personal pages are also where you're most likely to find hobbyists and others who share your more peculiar interests. The Web lets anyone publish, which means there might even be a few things that are interesting enough to read!

Most of the information in this book is geared towards helping you create snazzy-looking personal Web pages. Here's a list of information that commonly appears on a personal home page:

- Contact Information
- Hobbies
- Interests
- Occupation
- Personal Background
- Picture of yourself
- Publications
- Links to other neat Web pages

Tip

Many people create home pages and then put their URL on their business cards and resumes (I do). Not only does this demonstrate that they are technically savvy, but it also gives them a chance to lend a little personality to their business persona.

Business Pages

As more and more people jump onto the WWW, an increasing amount of businesses are also taking the plunge. Virtually every day a new large company or corporation announces its brand new site on the Web, and scores of smaller companies make their appearance as well.

Asked why they want to be on the Web, practically every company will answer the same thing, "It's a new, exciting marketing tool, and a great way to reach customers." The WWW offers an unprecedented opportunity for businesses and companies to get publicity and market their products and/or services for a relatively low cost.

Support

Companies such as Microsoft, Lotus, and IBM have recognized the potential to offer technical support to their customers via the WWW. Microsoft offers its technical knowledge and Lotus has its internal "white papers" all available through the Web (see fig. 2.1).

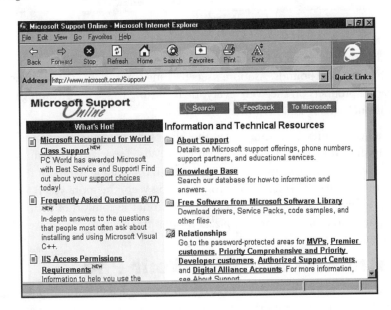

Fig. 2.1

Here's a sample of Microsoft's support site at **http://www.microsoft.com/Support/**.

Supporting customers on the Web has evolved into an effective and afford-able medium and more and more companies offer support over the Web every day.

Sell Products

Nowadays, you can buy virtually anything on the WWW. Whether you want an antique rocking chair, or clothing of the latest fashion, you'll find it on the Web (see fig. 2.2).

Fig. 2.2
Here's a familiar name that's doing some business on the Web (**http:// www.landsend. com/**).

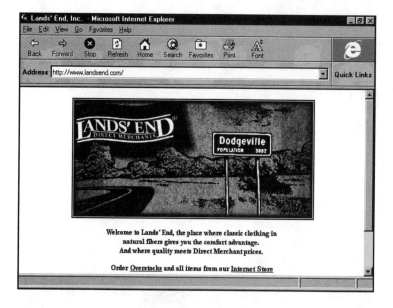

Apparently, selling products on the Web can be quite lucrative, and it's grow-ing by leaps and bounds. As more users become comfortable with the idea of ordering products on the Web, everyone is starting to see the advantages over traditional catalog and mail-order business.

Several companies have announced that their sales have increased signifi-cantly since they've had a presence on the WWW, especially companies that take Web commerce seriously, and understand the unique nature of the Internet shopper. The more you browse on the Web, the more you'll find an opportunity to spend money and buy items from the comfort of your own computer (you can even order a pizza through the Web in some places).

Gathering Ideas for Your Page

There are two aspects to evaluating every home page: content and presenta-tion. First, you have to decide what information to put on your home page.

Some people (like me) put personal information such as pictures and hobbies on their pages, while others only list their technical or business interests. You get to decide how much and what type of information you make available on the Web.

Don't worry if you can't decide exactly what to put on your home page. There are no wrong answers. Simply create your page, put it on the WWW, and see what other people think. The response you get from your original page will likely motivate you to update it in various ways.

Read this section to learn about different ways to organize and present your home page. You'll see several different home pages that actually exist, and some suggestions for how you can make your page top-notch. While I won't tell you exactly what to put on your home page, I will make some suggestions and show you some examples to help you along the way. As I do, I'll point out some of the good things you may want to include and some of the bad things you may want to avoid.

Short but Sweet—Roxanne's Page

This page is an example of how even an extremely simple home page can easily fit your needs, represent you adequately, and not take an overwhelming amount of time designing, planning, and maintaining.

Take a look at Roxanne's page (see fig. 2.3). She lists a few things that are important to her—taxes, coin collecting, and her cockatiel. What's great about this page is that it is easy to read and is well presented.

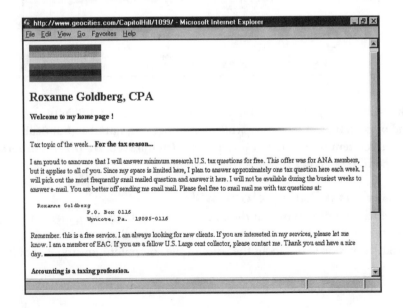

Fig. 2.3
Roxanne's page is easy to take care of, but there's not a lot of meat there (yet).

Stop by **http://www.geocities.com/CapitolHill/1099/** and see what
Roxanne is doing.

Intermediate Level—My Personal Page

Here's my own personal home page (see fig. 2.4). You might be surprised that
it doesn't have thousands of graphics, tons of links, and use every HTML feature discussed in this book. But, I have spent a lot of time organizing my page
to make it easy to use. I've also discovered that most pages that have an
abundance of graphics are often too confusing to communicate well. And,
I've endeavored to make my page viewable by nearly every Web browser on
the market, so I've stuck with HTML 2.0 standard tags, even when Netscape-
specific or HTML 3.2 tags would make things more attractive.

Fig. 2.4
My page repre-
sents an organized
home page with-
out adding too
many complicated
extras.

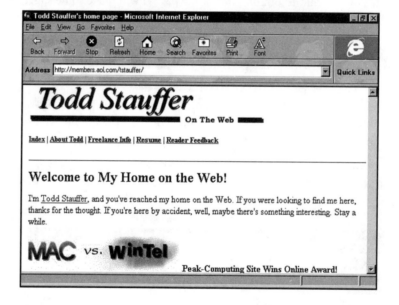

That said, my page is the next level up from Roxanne's in difficulty, design,
and presentation. It took me a while to put together, but it isn't difficult
to keep current or to add new information. On the Web, **http://members.
aol.com/tstauffer/** is where you'll find me.

Classy Web Page—clnet online

I spend a great deal of time at the clnet online site. Daily computer news
updates on the Web site add to clnet's Web-based radio programs and its
weekly television show about the latest in the computer industry. Part of it is

professional, and part of it is just plain fun. With a magazine-style format, clnet takes great advantage of the interactivity and technology available on the Web. It also has a huge staff for maintaining the site!

This site uses a nice combination of text, graphics, and organizational techniques for an all-around superb presentation. Exploring these pages, you'll find video clips, audio bites, and several images all related to clnet's primary mission—providing computer news.

Visit **http://www.cnet.com/** to see and learn the latest about computing on and off the Web (see fig. 2.5).

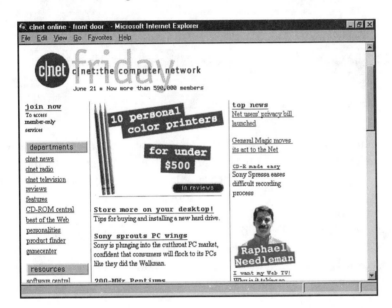

Fig. 2.5
clnet online is a great example of the next generation of Web-based magazine and multimedia content rolled into one.

Excellent Commercial Site—ESPN SportsZone

I've included a couple of other commercial sites so you could see what other types of pages look like. Commercial pages tend to be more impressive because they have more financial backing than individual home pages.

This site is ESPN's home page, titled SportsZone (see fig. 2.6). SportsZone offers an attractive format without any difficult-to-maintain HTML tricks. Every time you link to this page, you find the newest and latest sports information. That makes you want to come back again and again.

Fig. 2.6

ESPN's SportsZone talks about teams, trades, and tribulations affecting major league sports. (The mostly text mode is shown here.)

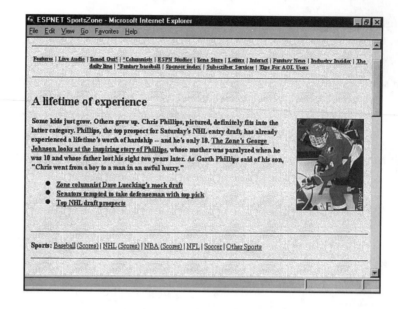

One of the keys to ESPN's presentation is the fact that it offers two ways to view the entire site—a "mostly text" presentation and a highly graphical interface. Depending on your patience and the speed of your Web connection, you can choose the site that works best for you. And, it also drives home an important point for Web designers like us—the large amount of information that constantly hits this page makes it one of the hottest spots on the Internet, regardless of the whiz-bang nature of the interface. Stop by and check out **http://espnet.sportszone.com/** and don't forget to try both the high graphics and mostly text options.

Fantastic Commercial Site—Coca-Cola

This is the place to stop by for a cool and interactive Web experience. One quick look and you know you're in for a treat (see fig. 2.7).

This site takes advantage of some of the most complicated features of Web publishing. Geared towards Netscape-compatible browsers, the site uses clickable graphics (where different spots of a graphic take you to different Web pages) and HTML forms, and its designers practice good design techniques.

One drawback to creating a site like Coca-Cola's is the amount of work it takes to maintain the Web site. Updates constantly have to be created and the information always needs to stay current. In addition, creating the maps and forms used can be a difficult process even for experienced programmers.

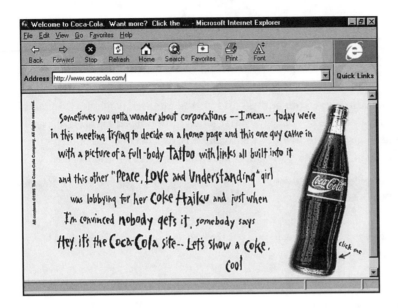

Fig. 2.7
It's fun looking at sites like this, but maintaining it by yourself would be a nightmare.

But when you're a company as wealthy as Coca-Cola, you can afford to hire folks who know what they're doing. Quench your thirst for exciting Web technology at **http://www.cocacola.com/** and, uh, smile!

Making Your Design Decisions

After finishing the whirlwind tour of the previously listed Web sites, you probably have lots of ideas for what you want to put on your home page. Before you dive in, though, you may want to take a few minutes to seriously consider what you're going to include. Just as an architect doesn't build without a blueprint, neither should you design a Web page without first figuring out what belongs where.

The first step is organizing the information you want to put on your page. I recommend organizing your home page into three distinct sections—personal, professional, and miscellaneous. After all, your goal is to put useful information about yourself on the WWW, and make it easy for visitors to find what they want.

It's a lot like how a house is designed. You'll have different parts of the house for different types of visitors. Formal living and dining areas might translate to the business side of your Web site. The family room and kitchen are similiar to the personal section, and everyone can explore your miscellaneous section, which might be like your backyard or garage. (At least, it might be like my backyard and garage, depending on how clean and organized you choose to make your site.) If everything was just listed together, visitors would have to read through your entire page before they find what they're seeking.

Then you'll need to break down each section even further. Decide whether you want to make your address and phone number available. Do you want to include a picture of yourself? What kinds of hobbies do you have? Visit my home page to see how I dealt with these issues. Feel free to "borrow" design ideas from my page or any other page that you like on the Internet.

Tip

Remember that you don't have to put everything on your home page on the first try. Spend your time putting a good but simple page (like Roxanne's) up there first. From there, you can increase your page's complexity.

Preliminary Page Design

Once you've started organizing your information, take some time sketching out how you want your home page to look. Just because the WWW is on a computer doesn't mean that good old pencil and paper can't help you out.

Draw your ideal page. Put your images, lines of text, and headlines all on your sheet of paper. I've found that drawing out Web pages (called "prototyping" in the design world) helps me think through the whole process. I know how big I want to make my images, how much text to type (approximately), what colors (if any) to use, and what kind of tables and lists I need to use (you'll learn more about these in Chapter 4). Don't be afraid to draw several sketches, even if they are very different (see fig. 2.8).

By adding this step to your Web page process, you're bound to put more thought into what information makes sense on a home page and how you want to present it.

For Which Browser Should You Design Your Site?

Here's another huge issue that will require a decision on your part. As I said in the last chapter, Netscape is the world's most popular browser, and hooks for using Netscape with the AOL service are rapidly coming to fruition. Hopefully, by the time you're reading this, it will be possible and easy to use the Netscape Navigator to access the Web via AOL. (Check out keyword **Netscape** for more information.)

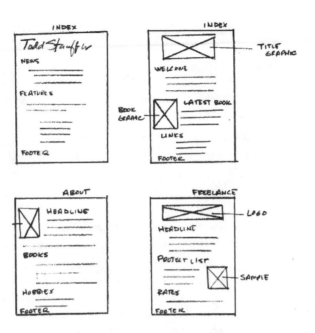

Fig. 2.8
Here are a few sketches of how I thought my home page could look.

But, Microsoft's Internet Explorer is the dominant Web technology for America Online users, and anyone who hasn't upgraded recently might be using AOL's even-older Web browser. Although Netscape and Internet Explorer control the vast majority of the Web browsing market, it's dangerous to assume that everyone on the Web has the same abilities to view pages as you do, especially the folks who don't use AOL for Web access.

It's really a difficult call to make. On one hand, using the least common demoninator (i.e., HTML 2.0 commands) lets the most people browse your site with the least amount of difficulty. Using Netscape, Internet Explorer, and HTML 3.2 commands, however, can make your page so much more fun to visit for folks who have the appropriate Web browsers.

Here's what I suggest. Since Internet Explorer is built into the latest versions of AOL, that will be our starting point. We'll discuss all of the latest tags from both Internet Explorer and Netscape, but I'll point out when we're talking about tags that not everyone can view. Beyond that, I'll leave the decision of which HTML commands to use up to you.

Tip

You've probably seen this before, but it's a great idea to add "Best Viewed in Netscape" or "Best Viewed in Internet Explorer" somewhere on your page if you use their special commands.

Want to Use Netscape with America Online?

As I've mentioned, the folks at America Online made a good move, in my opinion, when they licensed the Microsoft Internet Explorer software for use as the default AOL browser. Internet Explorer is a fine browser that supports most of the cutting-edge Web technology.

But, that doesn't mean you might not want to use Netscape Navigator for your Web browsing, and AOL has recognized that need as well. An agreement with Netscape Corp. has also made it possible for AOL to offer Netscape users a connection to the Web through the AOL service.

At the writing of this book, the latest version of Netscape was version 2.0.2, with version 3.0 waiting in the wings (currently in beta testing). Check out Netscape's Web site at **http://www.netscape.com/** for more information on Netscape Navigator.

In order to use Netscape with the AOL service as your connection you'll need to follow some special instructions. First, go to the special section on Netscape (keyword **Netscape**) in AOL's Internet Connection. There you'll find instructions for downloading Netscape (if necessary) and connecting to the Web through AOL.

In fact, using the special Winsock program designed for AOL, you can use a lot of third-party Internet applications (currently limited to 16-bit applications) through your dial-up AOL account. If you've ever wanted to run your own FTP, Internet Relay Chat, or similar program, try keyword **Winsock** for information and download areas that deal with using non-AOL Internet programs.

Double-Check Your Home Page with Another Browser

Although Netscape and Internet Explorer are much more popular than other browsers, it's always a good idea to see how your home page looks with another, perhaps less-capable, browser program. For all of the neat Netscape-compatible features you can use, you want your home page to be accessible to anyone who wants to browse it.

If you want to see your home page from another set of eyes, use Table 2.1 to locate and download other WWW browsers. Realize, however, that none of these browsers will currently run alongside AOL (unless you use only the 16-bit versions with the AOL Winsock add-on); but you can easily use these browsers to view the pages while they're on your hard drive. And that's a good idea. Testing your pages in one of the browsers listed in Table 2.1 will help you make sure you've done a good job for every potential viewer. If you have access to the older AOL Web browser, that's also a good choice for see-ing how less-capable browsers view your pages.

Table 2.1	Other Popular WWW Browsers and Their URLs
Browser	**Description/Location**
Mosaic	Developed at CERN, the original Web browser is similar to Netscape and is still updated consistently. Its address is **http://www.ncsa.uiuc.edu/SDG/Software/SDGSoftDir.html**.
Lynx	This is a text-based browser for workstations or other non-graphical environments, including DOS. Its address is **http://www.cc.ukans.edu/about_lynx/about_lynx.html**.
Arena	A browser designed to test new HTML standards, it currently runs only on UNIX computers. Its address is **http://www.w3.org/hypertext/WWW/Arena/**.

Tools for Creating AOL Web Pages

As I discussed in Chapter 1, HTML documents are text-based files that have special codes, called *markup tags*, within them. These markup tags tell WWW browsers such as Internet Explorer how to interpret and display text and graphics.

Since HTML documents are completely text, virtually any word processor or text editor from Windows Notepad to WordPerfect can be used to create a home page. The difficult part about creating HTML documents is remember-ing all the specific markup tags and learning how to use them properly.

AOL has an area called Personal Publisher that allows you to create very basic Web pages for display on the Web. If you like, you can get started immedi-ately with this service, and it requires that you learn no HTML codes. But the pages aren't much to look at. Once you're ready for some serious Web pages, we'll move on to more sophisticated tools, like HotDog.

Personal Publisher

AOL's Personal Publisher area is a simple tool for creating Web pages based on your Member Profile on America Online. It essentially allows you to say who you are, add a few lines of text and perhaps an image or two. It's not a bad place to start, especially if you're not sure that you want to go all out with HTML and the HotDog editor. At the very least, accessing the Personal Publisher area will let you put a Web page up very quickly—today, if you want (see fig. 2.9).

Fig. 2.9
Personal Publisher
is AOL's online
tool for creating a
very simple Web
page.

The Personal Publisher area (keyword **Personal Publisher**) uses a slightly different URL for your home page than does the standard AOL Web service. (You'll access your page with the URL **http://home.aol.com/ screenname/** if you use Personal Publisher.) It does eat into your 2 MB AOL Web space allowance, though, so if you plan a more involved page, you might want to forgo using Personal Publisher. Honestly, the page created by Personal Publisher won't be that large, but it's a little redundant if you'll be using the rest of this book!

We'll talk more about creating a home page with Personal Publisher in Chapter 3, "Building a Simple Web Page with AOL Online Tools."

Using HotDog for Advanced Web Pages

Personal Publisher lets you get a page up on the Web quickly, but there isn't much to it. That's what the rest of this book is about—creating better looking pages. For that, you'll probably want a good HTML editor application.

Several programs exist to make it easier to create and enhance your HTML documents. In this book, I use one of the best, HotDog. HotDog is shareware software that allows you to create incredible-looking WWW documents without knowing very much about HTML. You simply type in the text to appear on your home page and use HotDog's buttons to mark how that text should be formatted. You can even preview your document directly in Internet Explorer, Netscape, and other Web browsers you have handy. HotDog also provides many of the same functions as a standard word processor.

HotDog makes it easy for you to create your own home page and is included on the CD-ROM in the back of this book.

> **Tip**
>
> The version of HotDog included on the CD is a shareware version which is only good for 30 days (14 days for some versions). To use HotDog after that, you can buy the Standard edition for $29.95. HotDog Professional edition is a full-blown, impressive HTML editor that allows you to customize your HotDog icon bar, comes with several HTML templates, and may even support Java and VRML (see Chapter 9 for more information on those). The HotDog Professional edition will cost you $79.95 (newer versions may be more expensive). Either way, stop by the HotDog home page at **http://www.sausage.com/** for more information.

Read the next section to learn how to install and the basics of using HotDog to create your home page.

Installing the HotDog HTML Editor

HotDog version 2.53 (for Windows 3.1 or Windows 95) and HotDog 32-bit version 1.01 (Windows 95 only) can be found on the included CD-ROM. Simply insert the CD in your drive and follow these steps if you have Windows 3.1:

1. Choose File, Run.

2. Type **E:\apps\html\hotdog\hd251pro.exe** in the Run dialog box and press Return to load the Windows 3.x version. Make sure to replace the E drive with the drive letter for your CD-ROM.

If you are a Windows 95 user, follow these steps:

1. Choose Start, Run.

2. Type **E:\apps\html\hotdog\hd32app.exe** in the dialog box and press Return to install the 32-bit support files for HotDog.

3. After completing that installation, return to the Run item under the Start button and type **E:\apps\html\hotdog\hdinst.exe** in the Run dialog box and press Return. This will begin the installation process for 32-bit HotDog.

> **Tip**
>
> HotDog 2.53 will run very well in Windows 95, and is the exact same editor I used for this book. If you like, you can start with 2.53 and then move up to HotDog 32-bit's newer features later.

HotDog will walk you through the installation process and set itself up on your hard drive. Once installed, HotDog allows you either 30 days or 14 days of free use (depending on the version) until your license expires.

Once HotDog is installed on your computer, you've got to customize it so it can use Internet Explorer to preview your HTML documents. From the menu bar, choose Tools, Options to bring up the Options dialog box. Click the tab labeled File Locations to set your HotDog options. In the Preview Browser box, type the full filename and extension of where Internet Explorer resides on your computer.

Note

You could just as easily use Netscape or another browser as your Preview Browser. I'm suggesting Internet Explorer only because it's on the included CD and it's the main browser for AOL members.

Once you've typed the full path name and directory, click the Save Options button. (You can also click the icon directly to the right of the text box to browse for Internet Explorer.) HotDog is now linked to your browser.

Tip

Several other good HTML editors are included on the CD-ROM that came with this book. If you have extra time, take a few minutes to browse through and evaluate some of the others.

Make sure you stop by the HotDog home page at **http:// www.sausage. com/** to see if a newer version of HotDog is available for downloading (see fig. 2.10).

A Brief HotDog Tour

Once HotDog is installed in Windows 3.1, double-click the icon labeled HotDog Editor to begin the program. In Windows 95, choose Start, Programs and then click the HotDog icon once (assuming you added a Start menu shortcut when you installed HotDog). A shareware notice appears, and then the main editor window appears. The first time you use HotDog, a dialog box will come up asking you for your next action. Click the Use HotDog Now button to continue (see fig. 2.11).

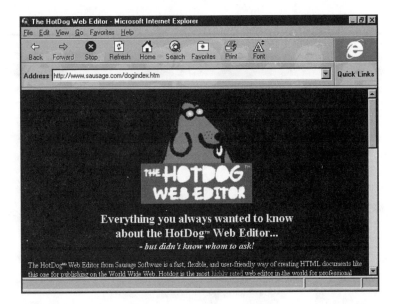

Fig. 2.10
The HotDog home page is fun to visit and is the clearinghouse for future releases of the editor.

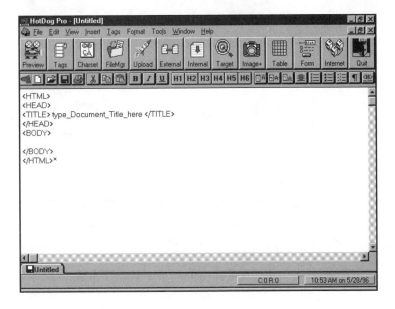

Fig. 2.11
Here's the main HotDog screen ready to go!

Table 2.2 describes the HotDog screen in further detail.

Table 2.2	HotDog's Button Bar Interface
Button	**Description**
Preview	Click to see a preview of your current HTML document in Netscape.
Tags	Click to choose from a number of drag-and-drop HTML tags.
Charset	Click to choose from a number of drag-and-drop special character formats such as bold.
FileMgr	Click to access the HotDog File manager, from which you can retrieve HTML, image, and other documents from your hard drive.
Upload	Click to upload files via FTP (not for AOL users).
External	Click to link your home page to other documents on the WWW.
Internal	Click to link highlighted text to specific targets in your home page.
Target	Click to create targets in your home page that you can link to (useful when you have a big home page).
Image	Click to create an inline image.
Embed	Click to choose a file to embed as a link within your document.
Table	Click to create a table within your HTML document.
Form	Click to add form elements to your document.
Internet	Click to insert hypertext links for Internet functions such as e-mail or FTP.
Quit	Click to quit HotDog.
Publish	Click to save your document and apply any special publishing options on your text that you set (Tools, Options).
Font	Click to add formatting to your document text.
Document	Click to set document-wide attributes such as background color.

You'll use the buttons lining the top of the screen to add new HTML elements to your home page. All you have to do is type your Web page text in the main window. Then, using your mouse, highlight the different parts of the text you want to change with an HTML command. Click the appropriate button and voilà, your text is marked automatically.

For example, type the following text in your main window:

Extra! Extra! Read all about it!

According to Fortune Magazine, Bill Gates is the second richest person in the world, second only to royalty who inherited his money from his family and past generations. Not to be outdone, Gates intends to buy his own country and set himself up as monarch for life.

Now take your mouse and highlight Fortune Magazine. We want to italicize that text because it is a magazine's title. So click the Italics button and watch HotDog add the <EM> and </EM> tags automatically for you. Now boldface Gates' name wherever it appears in the preceding paragraph by selecting the text and clicking the boldface icon. Finally, let's make the first line look like a headline. Select it and click the H1 button.

When you are finished, your text should look like this:

```
<H1> Extra! Extra! Read all about it! </H1>

According to <EM>Fortune Magazine </EM>, <STRONG>Bill Gates</STRONG>
is the second richest person in the world, second only to royalty who
inherited his money from his family and past generations. Not to be
outdone, <STRONG>Gates </STRONG> intends to buy his own country and
set himself up as monarch for life.
```

Now click the Browser Preview button. Internet Explorer appears and shows you how the text would look to people browsing on the Web (see fig. 2.12).

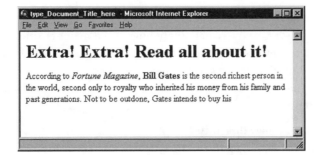

Fig. 2.12
Not too compli-
cated, but pretty
neat for ten
seconds of work.

Where to Put Your Web Pages

If you're reading this book in order you haven't learned a whole lot about creating Web pages yet. But, once you have, it'll be important to know how to actually send your pages to AOL so that they can be displayed on the World Wide Web. So, we'll talk about that quickly right now.

Once you've created Web pages, you've got to have access to a Web server so that other folks on the Web can view your site. For most Web designers, that means heading out to find a good Internet presence provider (IPP) company or Internet service provider (ISP) that's willing to sell them space on a Web server.

> **Note**
>
> In Internet lingo, an Internet service provider (ISP) provides a direct connection to the Internet for the user, allowing access to e-mail, UseNet, the WWW, and other services. An ISP might also provide Web server space, but not necessarily. On the other hand, an Internet presence provider (IPP) offers only server space—sometimes just Web server space, but often an IPP will offer FTP and Gopher server space as well.

Fortunately for us AOL members, we can skip that step—at least to start. America Online offers each of its users 2 MB of space on its members Web server for no extra charge. Plus, each AOL account can actually have up to five users associated with it, each of whom receives the 2 MB limit. So, theoretically, a single AOL account has up to 10 MB of Web space with which to work. For most of us, that's plenty. The trick is actually getting the pages organized and uploaded to your personal Web space on AOL!

Web Site Organization

Unless your site will be overwhelmingly huge (for a major business site, for instance), I'd recommend that you plan to leave all of your files in the same directory on America Online's server. Not only does that make it easier to upload your files, but it also makes it easier for you to test your Web site on your own computer.

Start by creating a new directory (WEB_SITE, for instance) on your PC for the Web pages you plan to create. Now, whenever you create a Web page in HotDog, you can save the HTML document to this directory. You can also save anything else you create for your Web site—multimedia files, graphics, sounds—to this directory. When you go to upload your files to AOL then, the task will be much simpler.

Viewing Pages Locally, First

This type of organization will also make it easier for you to test your Web site before uploading it to America Online. In fact, there's a straightforward process that you should generally follow any time you edit your site. It is as follows:

1. Create (or edit) your Web pages and save them to a special local directory you've created for the site.

2. Using your Web browser's File Open command, load the index.htm file into your browser. Using Internet Explorer 2.0 or higher, you can also enter the path to the file directly in the URL text box (e.g., **c:\web_site\index.htm**), as shown in figure 2.13.

> **Tip**
>
> You should always name the first (or only) HTML page at your Web site
> index.htm (or index.html on servers that accept long filenames, like AOL's Web
> server). Many browsers and Web server programs will automatically look for this
> file when it's necessary to access your site.

Fig. 2.13
Use your browser
to view your site
locally, before it's
uploaded to the
Web server.

3. Test all of the links by clicking them to make sure they properly load
    the associated Web page. Also check for typing errors and problems
    with graphic files.

4. If necessary, reedit your HTML documents to fix any errors or broken
    links. Then, retest.

Uploading Your Web Pages

Once you have your site working correctly when viewed from your hard
drive, you're ready to put it up on the Web. To do this, you'll access the My
Place area on the America Online service. Follow these steps:

1. Log on to AOL.

2. After you've successfully entered the AOL server, use the keyword **My
    Place** to access the special area for uploading Web files. The My Place
    dialog box should appear.

3. In the My Place dialog box, click the Go To My Place button.

4. The next window you see will be AOL's FTP interface to the **members.aol.com** server (see fig. 2.14). Notice that you're automatically pointing to a directory that uses your member name as the name of the directory (in all lowercase letters). To upload a file for your Web site, click the Upload button.

Fig. 2.14
Use the My Place FTP interface to upload HTML and multimedia files to your Web site directory on AOL's Web server.

5. In the Remote Filename text box, enter the name of the file you want to upload. If the file is a text file (e.g., an HTML document), click the button marked ASCII. If it's a binary file (e.g., a graphic or multimedia file), click the Binary button. Then click Continue.

> **Caution**
>
> Remember to give the file the exact name you used when creating the site. Otherwise, your hypertext links might not work correctly. If everything worked when you tested the site locally, you can use the exact names you used when saving the files to the Web directory on your hard drive. You may need to write the filenames down on a sheet of paper, though, since AOL requires you to type the filename before it allows you to browse for the file on your hard drive.

6. Now you should see the Upload File dialog box. Click the button marked Select File to browse your hard drive for the correct file (see fig. 2.15).

7. Select the file you want in the Attach File dialog box and click the OK button.

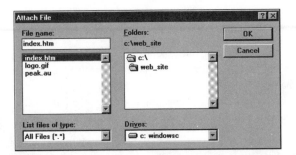

Fig. 2.15
Browsing for your Web files to upload is a lot like using the typical File, Open command in your other Windows programs.

Tip

If you get to this point and realize that you gave AOL the wrong filename, click Cancel and then click the Close box (upper right corner in Windows 95) to close the Upload File dialog box. You can then start over at step 4.

8. You are returned to the Upload File dialog box. Click the Send button. Your Web file will be uploaded to the AOL Web server (see fig. 2.16). When it's finished, you'll hear AOL say "file's done!" if your PC is sound-capable. You'll also see a File Transfer Complete message. Click OK.

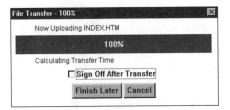

Fig. 2.16
This file is being uploaded to the AOL server.

And that's all it takes to send your file to America Online. In fact, it's now available on the Web for others to view. That's all it takes. Except, of course, you now have to go through the same process for all the remaining files you want to include on your Web site. (Notice that once you've started the process, you're back at step 4, ready to enter the name for the next file.)

Other Folders in Your My Place Directory

You may have noticed that AOL automatically creates a folder labeled *private* in your My Place directory. And, on top of that, there's a button on the FTP interface marked Create Directory. So what's the deal?

(continues)

(continued)

The private folder named is designed so that no one from the Web can access a listing of its contents. They can download files from the folder—but only if they know the exactly name of the file. They can only get the file if you tell them about it. To download the file secret.doc from my private directory, for instance, you'd use the URL **ftp://members.aol.com/tstauffer/private/secret.doc**.

To create a new directory, just click the Create Directory button and enter a name. You can create a directory for just about anything—perhaps a directory called images where you can store all of your graphic files for your Web site.

There is one special case for creating a directory. If you create a directory called incoming, AOL automatically assumes that you want folks on the Web to be able to upload to that directory. (Web users aren't permitted to upload to any other directory, including your main My Place directory.) You've got to watch that, though. If you let people upload to an incoming directory, it could run you up against your 2 MB limit.

Your AOL Web URL

With your files all properly uploaded to the AOL Web server, you're now ready to test the site as it will appear on the Web for everyone to see. To do this, you'll load the index page in your Web browser, and then test all the graphics and links.

One of the most important things you'll need to know to do this is where, exactly, your Web site is on the Web. The URL for accessing your Web site is just **http://members.aol.com/** plus the screen name you used when you uploaded files and a trailing slash, like **http://members.aol.com/ screenname/filename.ext**.

Using this URL, any one of your Web files can be accessed over the Web. Why is this the URL? AOL has created a directory on its Web server for each of your AOL screen names. For instance, my main screen name on the AOL service is **TStauffer**. So, when I use the My Place area to upload files (while I'm signed on to AOL as **TStauffer**), the files are uploaded to **http:// members.aol.com/tstauffer/**.

Now, if I have an HTML document named index.htm, the AOL Web server will automatically send the index file whenever a browser accesses the above URL. To directly access a file, we simply add that to the URL, as in **http:// members.aol.com/tstauffer/resume.htm**.

And that's all it takes! Everyone who uses the My Place area to upload files to the AOL Web server uses this same pattern.

Accessing the Site

Armed with an URL, you can now access your Web site with a browser to test it. Follow these steps:

1. Load your Web browser. If you're using AOL to access the Web, enter the keyword **Web**.

2. In the Web Address text box at the top of your Web browser's window, enter the URL for your site. (If you named a file `index.htm` when uploading, you don't need to enter a filename along with the URL. The index file will be loaded automatically.)

3. The page should load in your browser. Welcome to your Web site!

Now you're ready to test the site. Just view all of your pages to check for errors or graphics that don't seem to load correctly. You should also test all of your links to make sure that all of your Web files and pages are working correctly.

That's it! Now you're ready to start updating your site. Don't forget that one of the keys to a great Web site is keeping it up-to-date and changing it often. You may never sleep again! ❖

CHAPTER 3

Building a Simple Web Page with AOL Online Tools

One way to create a simple Web page—and get started right away—is using AOL's Personal Publisher area. Within minutes of accessing this area, you'll have a home page on the World Wide Web that you can call your own.

The Personal Publisher tools are rather limited, though, so this chapter isn't for everyone. If your first priority is getting a Web page up and running on the Web, then read on. If it's more important to you that your Web site is flexible, uses more advanced commands, and is generally more useful (whether for personal use or for your business), then you can skip this chapter and move right to Chapter 4, "The Web Page Basics."

What is the Personal Publisher Area?

The Personal Publisher area is a special area on America Online that allows you to create a basic home page without learning any of the HTML codes discussed in the rest of this book. It's a great way to quickly get a page up on the World Wide Web, but it's fairly limited in what it allows you to create. Personal Publisher allows you to add photos, links to other Web sites, and some personalized text; but, for the most part, all Personal Publisher Home Pages end up looking very similar.

Home Pages versus home pages versus starting pages

On the Web in general, the words "home page" have come to mean two completely different things. Many people say "home page" when they mean the page they've created on the Web that offers information about them, their personal hobbies, or their business.

(continues)

(continued)

Originally, however, the words "home page" were used to suggest the *starting* page that you accessed when beginning a Web session. It was the page that acted as the base of operations for your Web experience, with common or favorite links to get you going.

Personal Publisher is used to create what AOL calls a *Home Page*, and I've capitalized that throughout this chapter to try to avoid at least some confusion. Following the AOL defaults, the Personal Publisher is actually creating just a simple Web page that you can use for any reason. It can be both a "home" page for others to view and a "starting" page for your Web excursions.

If you do decide to create a starting page, then I'll show you how to set your Personal Publisher Home Page as the first page that loads in your AOL browser. That's in the section "Setting Your Home Page as the AOL Browser's Default Page" toward the end of this chapter.

How Personal Publisher Works

The page you create in Personal Publisher is based on the Member Profile you create for others to view on the AOL service. When you begin working in the Personal Publisher area, AOL automatically creates a basic page that uses your Profile information, like your name, birthday, hobbies, and personal quotes.

Tip

To access the Member Profile area on AOL, use the keyword **Profile** or access the profile directly with the menu command Mem_bers, My AOL and then click the Be Seen! button. (In versions of AOL before 3.0, choose Mem_bers, Edit Your Online Profile.)

The Personal Publisher then allows you to enter some special text on your page that you might want to use to describe yourself in more depth, talk about your hobbies, or even discuss your business. Then, you can add image files or links to other pages, multimedia files, or other places on the Internet.

The Home Page URL

As discussed in Chapter 2, AOL Web authors who use the My Place area to upload Web files have a special URL for accessing those Web pages. If you use the Personal Publisher area for your page, though, you'll use a slightly different URL. AOL still creates a new directory for your Web site, but it uses a different server computer, following the format **http://home.aol.com/ screenname**.

The *screenname* is your AOL screen name (in all lowercase letters). If I created a page for my main screen name, **TStauffer**, then the URL for my Personal Publisher Web page is **http://home.aol.com/tstauffer**.

This is the address that anyone with a Web browser and Internet access can use to view my Personal Publisher Home Page on the World Wide Web.

How You Get There

Personal Publisher is an area on the AOL service itself, although it does use the AOL Web browser for some of its functions. Once you've logged onto the server, you can get to Personal Publisher with the AOL keywords **Personal Publisher** or **Home Page**. You can also access the Personal Publisher area from the main menu of the Internet Connection (keyword **Internet**). Once there, the Personal Publisher menu gives you a couple of different options and resources (see fig. 3.1).

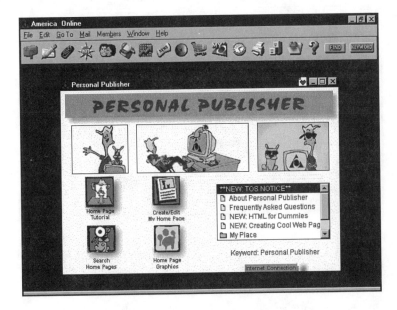

Fig. 3.1
The Personal Publisher area on AOL offers information and tools for creating a simple Web page.

Aside from creating your Home Page, you can also access the Personal Publisher Home Page Tutorial, search other AOL home pages, and go to a special Home Page graphics section. In fact, AOL offers some interesting services for making any of your Web pages more interesting. For instance, the PicturePlace area lets you use postal mail (called *snail mail* in Net lingo) to send regular snapshots, which PicturePlace will scan into electronic files for inclusion on your Home Page. There's also a special AOL area where you can select free graphic images for your Web pages. (We'll discuss both of these in Chapter 6, "Spicing Up Your Home Page with Graphics.")

Creating a Personal Profile Page

Our first priority is to get our Home Page up and running. To do that, we start at the Personal Publisher menu. Follow these steps:

1. Click the Create/Edit My Home Page button. This loads the Web browser and gives you access to the Create/Edit My Home Page tools (see fig. 3.2).

Fig. 3.2

The Personal Publisher tools use the AOL Web browser. Click the grow box to expand this page to fill the screen.

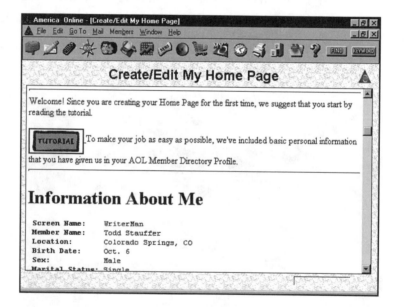

2. Notice that AOL automatically adds your Member Profile information to your Home Page (if you've created a Member Profile). Scroll to the bottom of this page and click the Create button.

3. Now you're ready to edit your Home Page. Scroll down to the Information About Me section (see fig. 3.3). This is actually a Web-based form that allows you to change your personal profile information. You can click in any text box to edit (or add) text for each category. Click the radio buttons (e.g., the buttons for Marital Status) to choose the options you want. If you don't want a particular option to appear on your page, don't enter any text.

Note

Editing this personal information for your Home Page also automatically updates your AOL Member Profile.

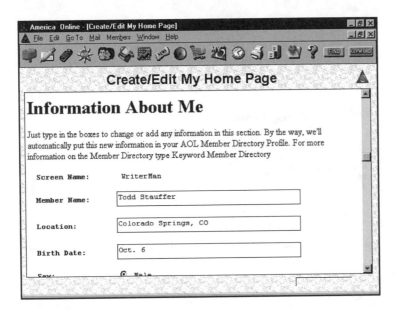

Fig. 3.3
Here you can edit your personal information for your Home Page.

4. When you're finished editing, scroll to the bottom of this page and choose whether the page will be viewable by the entire Internet, by just AOL members, or by only you. (You may want to make it viewable to only you until it's "ready" for others.)

5. Click the See My Changes button. Now you can see the information you've changed or added to your personal profile. This is how your information will appear on your Home Page (see fig. 3.4).

6. If you're satisfied with your progress thus far, click the Save Changes button. You've got a Home Page! (Follow the on-screen instructions to view your page.)

Once you've created your Home Page, AOL automatically changes its options so that these exact steps, if you perform them again, give you the option to Edit (instead of Create) your Home Page.

Adding Text to Your Page

Now that you've got your Home Page created and available to folks on the Internet (if you've chosen to do so), there's something you might have noticed about it. It's boring! We've got to have at least a little more than this electronic version of a personals advertisement, right?

Fig. 3.4
Here's how my Home Page will look now that I've entered my personal information.

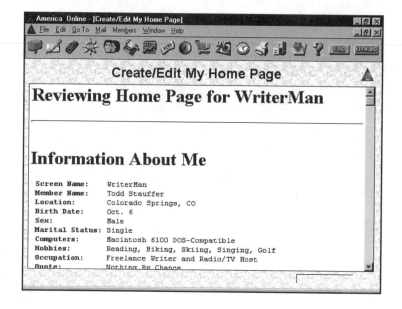

Fortunately, the Personal Publisher lets you add some freeform text to your page, too. You can type anything you want—welcome folks to your Home Page, talk about your kids, or discuss your business or hobbies. Here's how to add some text:

1. From the Personal Publisher menu, click the Create/Edit My Home Page button.

2. This should look familiar. Scroll to the bottom of the page, but this time click the Add button.

3. Now you're on the Add Links, Multimedia, and Text page of Personal Publisher. Let's start with adding text. Scroll down to the Add Text area (see fig. 3.5). Click in the text area and type the text you want to add.

4. When you've got your text the way you want it, scroll to the very bottom of the page and click the See My Changes button.

5. If you like what you see, click the Save Changes button at the bottom of this page.

If you'd like to add more text to your page, you can click the Add button again (instead of the Save Changes button) to add another paragraph.

You'll be back at the Add Link, Multimedia, and Text page again, and you can just follow the previous steps (starting with step 3).

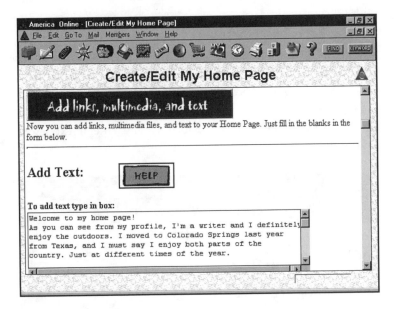

Fig. 3.5
Here you can add text to your Home Page.

Adding Images and Links

We've added a little text to our Home Page, and that's definitely a bit more exciting than the basic profile page. But isn't there more we can do? Well, the point of any home page is to link to other interesting sites on the Web. If you've got some favorites, you'll want to add them to your page for quick access—and to let other folks know about them.

Another major reason we use the Web is for the multimedia and images we can add, so we might as well try to spruce our page up a bit with some graphics, too, which we'll talk about in a moment.

Adding Links

Let's start by adding hypertext links to the page. Actually, the process is similar for adding both links and graphics, but we need to make a distinction between two different types of links first.

The first type of link is to another Web page somewhere on the Internet. To create this type of link, you'll need to know the correct URL for the link beforehand.

Here's how you add a link to an Internet URL:

1. From the Personal Publisher menu, click the Create/Edit My Home Page button.

2. Scroll to the bottom of the page and click the Add button.

3. Scroll past the Add Text area on this page to the Add Link section of the page.

4. To create the link, you need to do three things (see fig. 3.6.) First, use the pull-down menu to choose to make this a Web URL link. Then, enter the URL in the text box provided. Finally, enter a text description for this link.

Fig. 3.6

Add a link to another Web page using the Add Link area of Personal Publisher.

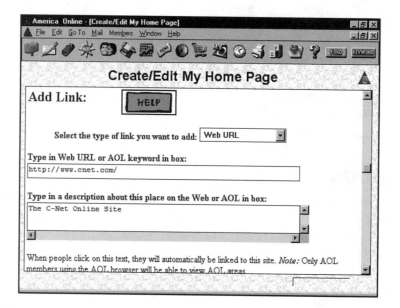

5. From here, you can scroll to the bottom of the page and click the See My Changes button. You'll be taken to the preview screen, where you should see the new link displayed below your personal info and any text you added previously.

If you'd like to add another link, you can scroll to the bottom of the preview page and click the Add button again. If you're happy with how things look, you can click the Save Changes button to move on.

> **Tip**
>
> Notice that the link is added right after the text you created previously. If you alter-
> nate between adding text and adding links, you can introduce each link with a para-
> graph of text, and then the link, if you'd like. (You can even alternate between text,
> links, and the graphics we'll add in the next two sections.)

Adding Links to Images

Here's the second type of link you can add. Instead of creating a link to another Web page, you may occasionally want your Home Page to display a
graphic image from another URL on the Web. For instance, you might want
to display your company's logo (stored on your company's Web site) on your
personal page. You can do this by linking to that graphic on your company's
site.

> **Caution**
>
> You should get permission before linking to a graphic on someone else's site. When
> you use the URL to a graphic file on another Web server, that distant server is actually
> accessed every time someone views *your* page. This might upset the owner of the
> remote site, since it puts a heavier burden on their server computers.

To add a link to a graphic file, follow the steps in the previous section, "Adding Links." When you're ready to add the link, choose Inline Image URL from
the Select The Type of Link You Want To Add pull-down menu (see fig. 3.7).
Then type the URL in the textbox below the menu.

The last step is to scroll to the bottom of the page and click the See My
Changes button.

Adding Graphics and Multimedia Files

Here's the last bit of customization you can perform on your Home Page.
In this last section, when we added graphics to our Home Page, we did so by
linking to a distant URL. This time, we'll actually upload the multimedia files
to our Web server space provided by AOL. So, while we do create a new link,
we're not accessing anyone else's site on the Web. The files are right there in
our Web space on AOL's server computer.

Fig. 3.7

Here's how to add an inline image from someone else's Web site to your Home Page.

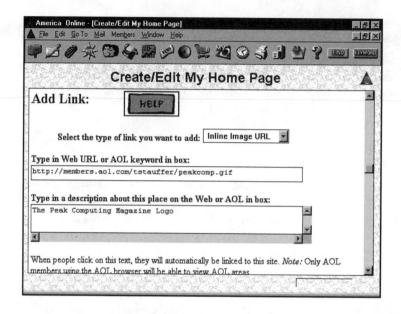

Adding local multimedia files is actually a two-step process—first we upload the file, then we add the multimedia file to our page. So what constitutes a multimedia file? A graphic image (like a GIF or JPEG graphic) a sound file (like .AU and .WAV files) or even QuickTime or AVI movie files. Any of these can be added to your page.

> **Note**
>
> Remember that AOL only allows you to have 2 MB worth of files stored for your Web site. Usually this won't be a problem, but multimedia files like sounds and movies can be *very* large. Check your file sizes to make sure you're not over the limit.

Follow these steps to add graphics and multimedia files:

1. From the Personal Publisher menu, click the Create/Edit My Home Page button.

2. Scroll to the bottom of the page, and click the Add button.

3. Scroll down the page until you get to the Upload Multimedia File section. Type the name of the file you want to upload, and then click the Upload Multimedia File button.

4. Now you'll see a page called Uploading File. Click the name for the file you just entered.

5. In the Upload File dialog box that appears, click the Select File button to browse for the file on your hard drive (see fig. 3.8.) Once you've found it in the Attach File dialog box, click OK.

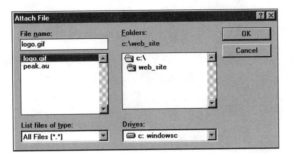

Fig. 3.8
Browse for the multimedia file to add to your Home Page.

6. You are returned to the Upload File dialog box. Click the Send button. The file will be uploaded to your Upload area. When it's finished, click OK in the File Transfer Complete box.

7. Now that the file is uploaded, we need to add it to the Home Page. Click the Add button again, and scroll down to the Add Multimedia File area.

8. Select the multimedia file you want to add in the menu. (If you've just started, there will only be one file.) Then type a description for the file, select a position on your page for the file (at the top of the page or after the other elements you've already added), and select how the file will be displayed. If it's an image file, you'll probably want it to display On Your Page. Other multimedia files (sounds and movies) should be added As A Link (see fig. 3.9).

9. When you're done, click the See My Changes button. That's how your page will look in a Web browser.

Now you can add more text, graphics, or multimedia files by clicking the Add button. When you've finished, click the Save Changes button. Then, move on to the next section of this chapter to take a look at your Home Page with the AOL Web browser.

Fig. 3.9
Once the multi-media file is uploaded, you've got to make some choices to get it on your page properly.

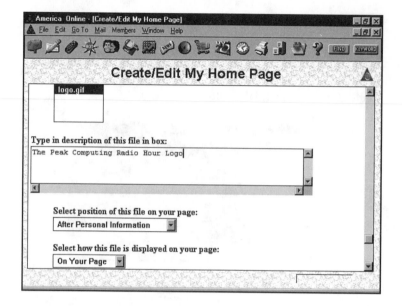

Viewing Your Home Page

Want to see how your page will look out there on the Internet? First, make sure you have selected the Save Changes button in the Personal Publisher and you've returned to the Personal Publisher main menu. Now it's just a matter of making your page available to the Internet community, firing up your Web browser, and entering the proper URL.

Changing Your Page's Availability

You won't be able to view your page with the Web browser if you haven't made it available for viewing on the Internet. If you recall, this was one of the first options presented to us when we created the page. Now, in order for everyone on the Web to see the final product, we've got to make it available for viewing. (If you chose to make it viewable by the entire Internet at the outset, then you can move on to the next section, "Loading Your Web Page in the AOL Browser.")

Here's how you change your page's status:

1. Select the Create/Edit button from the Personal Publisher main menu.

2. Scroll down to the bottom of the the Editing Home Page screen. Click the Edit button at the bottom of this screen.

3. On the next editing screen, scroll down past your personal information to the section You Can Choose Who Can View Your Home Page and click the radio button next to the AOL and Internet option.

4. Continue scrolling to the bottom of the page and click the See My Changes button.

5. Now you're seeing how the page will be formatted. Scroll to the bottom of this page and click the Save Changes button.

You'll be told that your page is saved and you'll be reminded of your page's URL. In fact, you can click the underlined link to go directly to your home page in the AOL browser. Otherwise, click the close box on this window to return to the Personal Publisher home page.

Loading Your Web Page in the AOL Browser
Our final step is to go directly to the AOL Web browser and see how our Home Page will look to the outside world. Follow these steps:

1. From anywhere on the AOL server, enter the keyword **Web** to load the Web browser.

> **Tip**
>
> As the browser loads, you might choose to click the Stop button before the AOL main page finishes loading, just to save time.

2. In the Web browser's URL text box, enter the URL for your home page, following the format **http://home.aol.com/*screenname*** (substitute your actual AOL screen name for ***screenname***).

What next? You should be viewing your own Home Page now through AOL's Web browser (see fig. 3.10). This is your calling card to the Internet, so you better check it for typos, unloaded graphics, and other similar problems. If you're happy with everything, you're done!

Setting Your Home Page as the AOL Browser's Default Page
Although most people see their home page on the Web as a way to communicate with other people, the original purpose for the home page was to serve as a starting point for the creator (hence the term "home"). The idea is that you'd create your own page with your favorite links and frequently accessed sites.

Well, that's still possible—and often a good idea. If you use this chapter to create or edit a home page that you feel will be useful for your Internet endeavors, then you can set your browser to load this page at the beginning of your Internet sessions.

Planning Your Web Page

Fig. 3.10
Viewing the
finished Web page
through AOL's
Web browser.

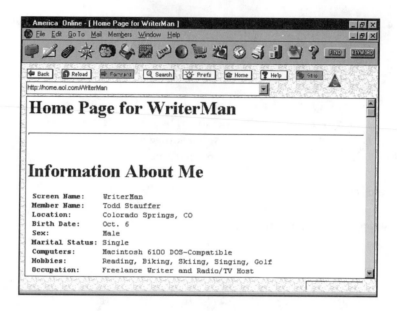

Here's how to set your home page as the default page for the AOL Web browser:

1. Choose Members, Preferences.

2. Click the button marked WWW. The WWW Preferences dialog box appears.

3. At the bottom of the WWW Preferences dialog box, change the URL in the Home Page textbox to **http://home.aol.com/***screenname* (substitute your actual AOL screen name for *screenname*).

4. Click OK in the WWW Preferences dialog box.

5. Click the close box in the Preferences window.

Now, whenever you load the AOL Web browser, it will automatically load your home page as its default page. If you like, you can go back and edit the page in Personal Publisher to add more of your favorite URL links.

Deleting Your Home Page

There's probably two major reasons you might want to delete your page—you're creating a more sophisticated page using AOL's My Place area (and you don't want this other one hanging around not getting updated), or you've decided that it's time to completely start over. Either way, deleting your home page is easy enough to do.

To delete your home page:

1. Select the Create/Edit button from the Personal Publisher main menu.

2. Scroll down to the bottom of the Editing Home Page screen. Click the Delete button at the bottom of this screen.

3. If you're sure you want to delete your home page, click the Delete button again on the Warning screen.

4. Your page has now been deleted. To close the window, click the close box in the upper right corner.

Once you've deleted your home page, you can return to the Personal Publisher as if you'd never done any of the work in this chapter, and begin again by creating your home page.

The only difference is that AOL still remembers any personal information you entered when creating your page, and your AOL Member Profile (to access, choose Members, My AOL and then click the Be Seen! button) remains updated with any information you added during your initial go-around with Personal Publisher. ❖

Part II

Creating a Basic Web Page

CHAPTER 4

The Web Page Basics

You'll hear people who dabble in HTML called "HTML programmers" every once in a while, but I don't like that. Depending on the way you approach your Web pages, I'd rather that you call yourself an HTML author or an HTML designer. Why? Because HTML isn't anywhere near as complicated as most computer programming languages. And the focus on learning HTML shouldn't be the codes and rules—it should be what you can create with HTML.

It's much more important to get useful, meaningful words and stimulating graphics on your Web page than it is to make sure you've got the little codes all lined up neatly. So that's what we'll focus on as we learn the basics of creating Web pages.

Using the Standard Web Page Template

I have included a sample Web page template on the CD that comes with this book. This sample template contains tags preformatted for a simple, but elegant Web page. All you need to do is add your own text!

Feel free to use, customize, and modify the Web page template to your heart's desire. It's meant to be flexible to your needs, not rigid.

Although the template is included, we don't spend much time using it in this book. Instead, I'll show you how to use HotDog to mark up text from scratch. You'll learn how I built the template, how to use HTML tags, and what design decisions I've made.

Important HTML Tags

No matter what your page looks like or what kind of information you want to display, there are five HTML tags that every page should have so they follow HTML and WWW standards. They are as follows:

- **<HTML>**—Informs the browser that this document is written in HTML
- **<HEAD>**—Labels the introductory and heading part of the HTML document
- **<TITLE>**—Gives a title for the Web page, which is displayed at the top of the browser window
- **<BODY>**—Marks where the body text and information appears
- **<ADDRESS>**—Contains an e-mail address to get further information about a particular Web page

These tags don't really affect how your Web page appears. But, they are vital, since they tell the user's Web browser how to recognize different parts of the HTML document. They can also be used by special applications on the Web.

For example, your Web server might run a program that looks at every HTML document and tries to create a large listing of them. It might only list the text that appears in the <HEAD> tag because that's where the title of the document should go. So, if your Web page doesn't use the <HEAD> and </HEAD> tags, you wouldn't be included in the listing. In general, while they don't affect how your Web page looks, using these tags is considered proper.

Note

By default, WWW pages created with HotDog automatically have the <HTML>, <HEAD>, <TITLE>, and <BODY> tags in them, so you won't have to type them in yourself. You will have to add the <ADDRESS> tag yourself. And, you'll need to enter all of these tags in some other HTML editors and whenever you use a plain text editor (like Windows Notepad) to create HTML documents.

The *<HTML>* and *</HTML>* Tags

This tag is important because it tells browsers to interpret all the text enclosed by these tags as HTML text. Since HTML documents are strictly text-based, the <HTML> tag lets the user's browser know that a file is written in Hypertext Markup Language.

To use these tags, you'd put the <HTML> tag at the very top of your file. It should be the first typed text on your screen. Then you'd type its companion tag </HTML> at the very end of the file. All the text surrounded by these tags is now marked as written in HTML format. Did you notice the / in the second tag? The forward slash is used to indicate ending HTML tags. Most HTML tags come in pairs, surrounding the text they mark up. The closing tag of a pair will always start with a forward slash.

In fact, in HTML lingo, this type of a tag is called an *enclosing tag*, or a *container tag*, since it's designed to act on the text that it encloses. A single enclosing tag actually required two physical tags—an "on" tag and an "off" tag. In almost every case, the off tag is exactly like the on tag except for a leading slash (/).

So far, your Web page would look like this:

```
<HTML>
</HTML>
```

The *<HEAD>* and *</HEAD>* Tags

The next set of tags you'd want to include are the <HEAD> and </HEAD> tags. These tags identify and mark information in your HTML document that serves as the document's header, or title information.

Adding these tags to your Web page is just as easy as the <HTML> tags. You'd type **<HEAD>** on the screen in between the <HTML> tags and then type in its companion tag, **</HEAD>**, on the following line.

The *<TITLE>* and *</TITLE>* Tags

The Web page title is displayed in the Web browser's title bar when a user views the page. Additionally, it is the page's title that is saved in the Web browser's bookmark list.

Your title belongs within the <HEAD> and </HEAD> tags on your Web page. You can only have one title per HTML document. You may notice that HotDog has already created a set of <TITLE> tags for you—just type the title of your page between the <TITLE> and </TITLE> tags, such as:

```
<TITLE>Todd Stauffer's home page</TITLE>
```

Now click the Preview button from HotDog to bring up your Web browser to test the title (see fig. 4.1).

II

Creating a Basic Web Page

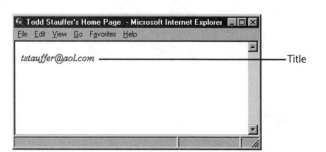

Fig. 4.1
Your title is an important label for your Web page.

Make sure you type a short, to-the-point, informative title.

Tip

Bad Web page titles are wordy, lengthy, and non-specific.

Titles should fit within the browser's title bar, be easy to reference, and accurately describe the site they represent. Good Web page titles might include the following:

- Todd Stauffer's Home Page
- Stauffer's Web Page
- Todd's Home on the Web
- Todd's Windows 95 Shareware Resource

Some bad Web page title examples are:

- My Page
- This is the fantastic, wonderful place to visit on the Web with lots of neat links and graphics
- Home Page, Sweet Home Page

The more specific the title is about the person, organization, or subject matter of the page, the more useful it is for users and specialized search engines. Generic names (and very long names) like the second series of examples aren't of much use to anyone.

The *<BODY>* and *</BODY>* Tags

Just like the <HEAD> tags, the <BODY> and </BODY> are used to create a separate section of your HTML document. Text surrounded by the <BODY> tags is the meat of your document. This area represents nearly everything that will be displayed in a browser's window.

Between the <BODY> tags is where most of your text and information will be typed because they are part of the document's body. Add <BODY> and </BODY> to your Web page and now your entire document looks like this:

```
<HTML>
<HEAD>
</HEAD>
<BODY>
</BODY>
</HTML>
```

The <*ADDRESS*> and </*ADDRESS*> Tags

We've discussed three sets of tags for your Web page, but we've entered no actual text yet. Now we'll add the <ADDRESS> tags, and this time we'll need to use HotDog to create the tags. The <ADDRESS> tags contain information about who to contact regarding this particular page. It is important to always put some kind of contact information on a Web page in case someone has a question or comment he or she wants to ask you.

The <ADDRESS> tag is used to separate that important information from the regular text body. Follow these steps to add the <ADDRESS> tag to your Web page:

1. In between the <BODY> and </BODY> tags, type your name and e-mail address. For example: **tstauffer@aol.com**.

2. Using your mouse, highlight the text you just typed and click the Tags button to bring up the available tags window (see fig. 4.2).

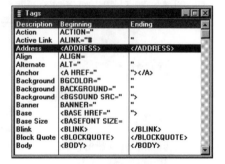

Fig. 4.2
HTML tags that you can drag onto your Web page are listed here.

II

Creating a Basic Web Page

3. Double-click the Address tag. HotDog automatically adds the <ADDRESS> and </ADDRESS> tags for you around your text.

Tip

You can also drag-and-drop tags directly onto your HTML document from the Tags window.

Figure 4.3 shows you how our HTML document looks so far in HotDog.

Fig. 4.3

Here's how our Web page stands in HotDog.

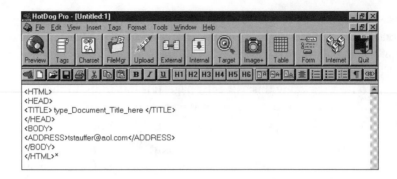

```
<HTML>
<HEAD>
<TITLE> type_Document_Title_here </TITLE>
</HEAD>
<BODY>
<ADDRESS>tstauffer@aol.com</ADDRESS>
</BODY>
</HTML>×
```

Caution

Even though you're just getting started, save your HTML file now with the File, Save command. Save frequently and regularly so you don't accidentally lose your work if your computer is hit with a power surge or if Windows or another program crashes or freezes your PC. When you save, your filename appears in the HotDog title bar.

Creating Headlines

Once you have all the basics in place, your next step is to add a headline that will appear on your Web page. Headlines are similar to titles in that they should be succinct and useful. Headlines come in six different sizes (creatively numbered one through six, with one being the largest). Figure 4.4 shows how the different headline sizes look in Internet Explorer.

Fig. 4.4

Here's how the six different headline sizes stack up against each other.

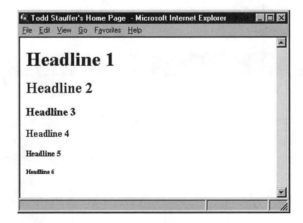

In most browsers, headlines appear larger and bolder than standard text and are a great way to divide your Web page into sections.

To use a level 1 headline on your Web page, you would use the <H1> and </H1> HTML tags to contain your headline text. Try adding a headline to your current page. Make sure that your text falls within the <BODY> and </BODY> tags. Follow these steps:

1. Type your headline text onto your Web page. For example: **Thanks for Visiting Todd's Web Site**.

2. Highlight your text with your mouse.

3. Click the button labeled H1 in the HotDog button bar at the top of the screen. Headline tags appear and automatically surround your text, like the following:

    ```
    <H1>Thanks for Visiting Todd's Web Site</H1>
    ```

4. Adding a secondary headline is just as easy. On the next line after your level 1 headline, type a secondary line of information, highlight it, and click the H2 button. For example:

    ```
    <H2>Have a Good Time!</H2>
    ```

5. Click the Preview button to see your Web page in your Web browser (see fig. 4.5).

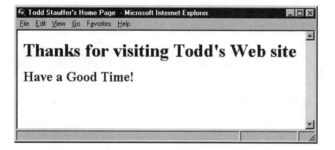

Fig. 4.5
Here's how Internet Explorer sees my Web page, headlines and all.

I use headlines to organize the different subsections of my Web page. As a general rule of design, if you use two headlines right after each other, only change the headline level by one increment (go from level 1 to level 2, or level 3 to level 4). This makes the transition from one level of text to the next appear natural to the eye.

Note

There's also a school of thought that claims that the most appopriate use of HTML headlines means never skipping a particular size. For instance, some folks believe that it's bad design if your first headline is anything smaller than an <H1> level headline. I personally feel free to start my pages at any level I feel appropriate. I've never encountered a browser program that cared one way or the other.

Creating a Basic Web Page

II

Adding Text to Your Page

With your Web page properly headlined, let's add some information that tells your visitors more about you. Adding text to your Web page is arguably the easiest step in the Web page creation process, since you can type directly into HotDog, and the text you type will display as normal text when viewing it with your Web browser.

Here's the paragraph of text I've used to introduce my own Web site for a number of months now:

> I'm Todd Stauffer, and you've reached my home on the Web. If you were looking to find me here, thanks for the thought. If you're here by accident, well, maybe there's something interesting. Stay a while.

Tip

Browsers ignore returns and extra spaces in paragraphs of text, so you can hit Return at the end of a line in HotDog if it makes it easier for you to read.

After typing that text, I can press the Preview button to see how it looks in Internet Explorer (see fig. 4.6). Then I can do whatever editing is necessary and save the page when I've finished.

Fig. 4.6
Here's how all the text comes out in Internet Explorer.

Breaking Text into Readable Chunks

Once you start adding text to your Web page, you'll soon realize that Web browsers don't display your text exactly the way you type it in an HTML editor. For example, the following text appears like this when typed into HotDog:

```
Here's a list of things I like to do in my spare time:
* Read books
* Travel
* Surf the Internet
* Enjoy live theater
```

That makes sense, doesn't it? We're just creating a simple list. But, it looks quite different when viewed in Internet Explorer (see fig. 4.7).

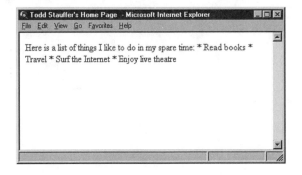

Fig. 4.7
All the text
jumbles together.

That's because the Web browser only formats information according to your markup tags. And Web browsers, by rule, ignore white space between paragraphs and returns that you add by pressing Enter or Return when you're typing. To create new lines of text or new paragraphs in HTML, you have to use special tags.

Caution

Web browsers require that you use special HTML tags to create line breaks, extra spaces, and space between paragraphs of text.

There are three basic tags you'll look at that help you break up text. With them you can create paragraphs, insert line breaks, and add horizontal lines between sections of text.

Unlike the tags we've discussed so far, these are not container tags—instead, we call them *empty tags*. Since they do something completely on their own (e.g., adding a line or extra spacing), they don't have to contain any text to act upon. In fact, empty tags don't even have "on" and "off" tags. Only one tag without a slash (/) is required.

The Paragraph Tag

The paragraph tag (<P>) tells the browser to separate two paragraphs of information with a blank line between them. It's useful when you have many paragraphs of text in a row.

Adding a paragraph tag is simple in HotDog. Place your cursor in the spot you want to have a tag and click the paragraph button (¶) in HotDog's button bar. A <P> tag is inserted automatically.

> **Tip**
>
> You don't have to use the paragraph tag to separate headlines, lists, and horizontal rules from text. By definition, the browser automatically includes an extra line of space before and after those HTML elements.

The Line Break Tag

The line break tag <BR> is similar to the paragraph tag, except that it does not add an extra line between the text it separates. After the tag, text continues directly at the beginning of the next line.

With HotDog, you can add the <BR> tag by moving your cursor to the correct position and clicking the <BR> button in the HotDog button bar.

I use the line break tag when I am creating a short list of items, like the following:

```
<H3>My Favorite Movies, in order:</H3>
Back to the Future<BR>
When Harry Met Sally<BR>
Field of Dreams<BR>
Midnight Run<P>
```

Notice that I used the <P> tag at the end of my list to separate it from the next paragraph (see fig. 4.8).

> **Note**
>
> Netscape-compatible browsers also support the word break tag <WOBR>. Rarely used, the word break tag allows you to definitively split words onto two separate lines. Just select Word Break from the list of available tags after clicking the Tags button in HotDog.

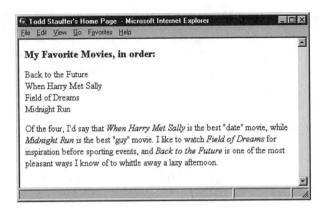

Fig. 4.8
My favorite movies, now available in HTML (for a limited time only).

Horizontal Rules

Vertical bites! (Okay, bad joke.)

The horizontal rule tag, <HR>, is one of the most useful and elegant tags available to help you separate and break up your Web page.

Adding this tag to your HTML document creates a line that goes across the screen in the user's browser. This line is useful for logically separating different parts of your Web page from each other.

I use the horizontal rule tag as an organizational and design tool. It helps people who view my Web page understand which pieces are related to each other, and it also separates my page into different sections. For example, I use the <HR> tag right above my e-mail address on my Web page to split that information apart from the regular text on my Web page.

You can use the <HR> tag anywhere within your HTML document's body. To add a horizontal rule tag, place the cursor in the document where you want the line and then click the Tags icon in HotDog's button bar. Scroll through the list until you get to Horizontal, and then drag that entry onto the document. You've added the line (see fig. 4.9).

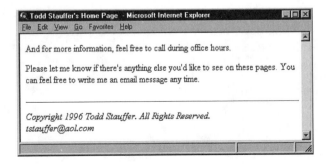

Fig. 4.9
I use the <HR> tag to keep my page shipshape.

II

Creating a Basic Web Page

Netscape-compatible *<HR>* Extensions

Bored with the standard <HR> tag, Netscape decided to spice up what you could do with the horizontal rule. It realized that a thin line across the page is useful in some cases, but occasionally you might want to have a different type of line. So it came up with a method for customizing how long your line is, how thick of a line displays, and how your line is aligned when viewing with Netscape and compatible browsers.

To add a horizontal line with special characteristics, follow these steps:

1. Place the cursor at the point in the document where you want the line to appear.

2. Choose Insert, Horizontal Line. This results in the Horizontal Rule dialog box (see fig. 4.10).

Fig. 4.10
You have lots of options for how your horizontal line appears.

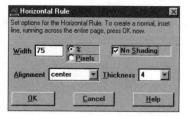

Here are the basic options for a Netscape-compatible horizontal line:

- **Width**—You can choose a percentage or an absolute value for how long your line appears in your Netscape window. I recommend always using a percentage value.

- **No Shading**—Lets you decide if your horizontal line appears solid black or as a shaded line (the default setting).

- **Alignment**—Determines how the line is aligned on your screen. You can choose left, center, or right from the drop-down menu bar. This feature is only useful when you specify the line width as well.

- **Thickness**—Sometimes you want a thicker line to separate your text. From the drop-down box, you can choose ten different thicknesses (2 is the default). It is extremely effective when you select the No Shading box as well.

Figure 4.11 shows several different types of horizontal rule lines.

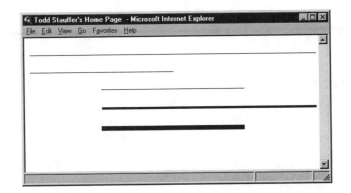

Fig. 4.11
These are examples
of many different
lines using
Netscape's HR
extensions.

Choose the specific options for your HR line and click the OK button.
HotDog will create the HTML code for you automatically and insert a customized line for you.

Note

As with many Netscape-specific tags, these special horizontal rule properties can only
be viewed by a handful of browsers, including Internet Explorer. Fortunately, most
other browsers just ignore them, so you can use them without worrying too much.

Preformatted Text

Sometimes you don't want the browser to take care of the formatting for you.
You may want to type some information into HotDog and have it look exactly the same in the user's browser, without worrying about paragraph tags.

In that case, use the <PRE> and </PRE> tags for preformatted text. Any text
that appears within the <PRE> tags will appear exactly the same in a browser—
spaces, hard returns, and all.

Add the <PRE> tags to your Web page by clicking the Tags button in HotDog
and choosing <PRE> from the available list of tags. See the section "Table
Alternatives" in Chapter 5 for more information (and an example) of using
preformatted text on your Web page.

Add Style to Your Text

The last section of this chapter deals with adding special formatting features
to your text. Sometimes you might want to emphasize a specific word or italicize a phrase. Other times you may want to center a headline, or even make
text stand out by having it blink intermittently.

Several text formatting features are available; some work with all browsers, and others only work with Netscape. Either way, these features can really add life to a Web page.

Centering

Centering is a great way to add a professional touch to your pages. Using the center tags <CENTER> and </CENTER>, you can make specific text and headlines stand out easily.

I like to use the center tags for my headlines, so they span the area where text appears, instead of being trapped on the left margin. To center text, highlight the area with your mouse and click the Center icon in HotDog.

The center tags appear around the text you've highlighted. Try centering your main Web page headline. After adding the tags, my HTML code now looks like this:

```
<CENTER><H1>Welcome to Andy's Home</H1></CENTER>
```

You can center headlines, horizontal lines, and paragraphs of text. In fact, once you learn how to add graphics, you can even use the <CENTER> tags to center the graphics on your page. Pretty much anything—even an entire page—will work between the <CENTER> tags.

Blinking Text

Blinking text is annoying, overused, and Netscape-specific. There's no good reason to use it, unless you want your page to look like the Web's version of a TV infomercial. Still interested? Just put the text between a <BLINK> and </BLINK> tag, like this:

```
<BLINK>Doesn't this look annoying?</BLINK>
```

Most Web designers consider the use of blinking text to be bad form.

Bold Text

You can mark various words and phrases in your HTML document to be displayed in boldface using the <B> and </B> tags. Text surrounded by these tags appears darker and thicker then standard text, and stands out nicely on your Web page.

Select text to be bolded and click the Bold button in HotDog. The bold tags appear around that text.

> **Note**
>
> You can also mark text to be darker by using the <STRONG> and </STRONG> tags. The strong tags are a more general term that tells browsers to make the marked text appear stronger on-screen. The strong tags are inherited from the parent language of HTML (SGML), but are not used as often now because each browser interprets what strong text means, creating some discrepancies. All graphical browsers recognize the bold <B> tag. Realize, though, that text-based browser applications *don't* recognize the bold tag, but they do understand <STRONG>.

Italics

Marking some text to be italicized is just as easy, only you use the <I> and </I> tags instead. HotDog makes it easy to mark italicized text by using the Italics icon on the menu bar.

> **Note**
>
> Similar to the strong versus bold debate outlined above, you can also emulate italics with other tags. The <EM> and </EM> tags, short for *emphasis*, make marked text stand out typically by italicizing the text. The <EM> tags are used more often than the <STRONG> tags, but their use is dwindling.

Once you're done adding all these emphasis tags to your HTML document, it starts to look a little complicated. Figure 4.12 shows you what everything is starting to look like in HotDog.

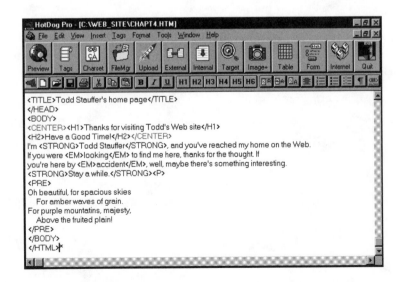

Fig. 4.12
HotDog, by default, inserts the <EM> for italic text and <STRONG> for bold tags.

The truth is, though, we've gotten pretty deep into text markup for our Web pages. Check out figure 4.13 and you'll see that we've actually begun to put together a fairly impressive Web page.

Fig. 4.13

Here are the same tags in Internet Explorer.

CHAPTER 5

Adding Lists and Tables to Your Web Page

One reason people like watching the nightly news is the amount of information that gets packed into 30 minutes. The newscasters realize that they've got to keep the viewers' interest or the viewers will switch channels. The news, then, needs to be in easy-to-access, digestible chunks.

Your Web pages need to follow this same practice. You have to organize your page and present your information in a concise and logical way, or users will leave your page faster than clicking on the remote control. With a simple Web page underneath your belt, it's time to start exploring different HTML elements that can help you organize your page and present information more attractively.

This chapter teaches you how to add lists and tables to your Web page. Lists and tables are HTML elements that make it easy to display groups of related information together in an easy-to-use format. You'll use lists to show itemized elements listed in order, while tables use a familiar row and column feel which allows you to display a lot of information in a concentrated area.

Although not difficult to use, lists and tables require a more thorough knowledge of HotDog and HTML.

What are Lists and Tables?

Nowadays, lists are an integral part of virtually any Web page. With several different types available, lists allow you to separate pieces of text and information outside of the standard paragraph format. While a paragraph wraps text around line after line in a traditional format, lists show text differently. Items in a list are indented, separated from other paragraphs of text, and usually preceded with a bullet or number.

Proper use of a list makes a large amount of information readable, usable, and easy to spot on a home page. Additionally, lists can be embedded within each other to allow you to display data in outline format. Personally, I use lists on my Web site to itemize my interests and organize the hotlinks.

Related to lists, tables use a row and column format to place information on your Web page. Supported only by Netscape and HTML 3.x browsers, tables are relatively new to the WWW.

Tables are fantastic for displaying a lot of related information in a usable format that fits on your screen. Anything that you would organize in columns makes sense to use a table. Companies commonly use tables to show products and pricing information, and many enthusiasts use Web pages to offer tons of links to related items.

Both tables and lists offer specialized formatting options (especially with Netscape-compatible extensions) to let you customize how they appear on your Web page.

What Lists Help You Accomplish

First off, I am going to show you what lists are and how you can use them on a Web page. Lists are extremely popular and can make a good Web page look great when used correctly.

I like to use lists in three major situations:

- When I have similar information that needs to be categorized in some fashion
- When I have a lot of data that would be too wordy and unreadable in paragraph format
- When I have a step-by-step process that needs to be described in order

Organize with Lists

Lists make it extremely easy to itemize information in a concise format. You don't have to bury important information inside of a long paragraph. Instead, use a list.

Take my home page as an example (**http://members.aol.com/tstauffer**). Originally, I had two paragraphs that described my own personal interests:

```
So what sort of stuff does Todd do? I'm a freelance book author,
with credits that include <EM>Using Your Mac</EM>, <EM>Using the
Internet with Your Mac</EM>, <EM>Easy AOL</EM>, <EM>SE Using the
Internet With Your Mac</EM> and <EM>SE Using Netscape 2</EM>.<P>

Aside from that I'm also a magazine columnist with <EM>Peak
Computing Magazine </EM>, Radio Host for the <STRONG>Peak Computing
Hour</STRONG> on the All-New Memories 740 in Colorado Springs, a
freelance business writer and, in my sparetime, an avid golfer,
among other things.
```

Not only were the paragraphs too wordy, but they presented a bunch of information in an unorganized fashion. Figure 5.1 shows the same information in list format, and figure 5.2 is how Internet Explorer displays it.

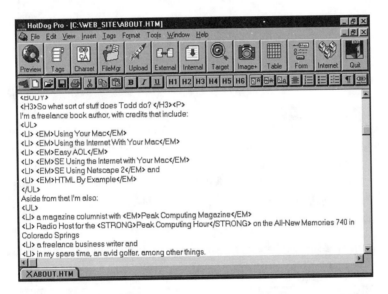

Fig. 5.1

Here's my personal interest list shown in HotDog.

II

Creating a Basic Web Page

Lists help you get information organized and make people more likely to read through your home page, because they can scan through a list and find what they are seeking. It also makes it easier to add hypertext links to these list items a bit later. And lists of links are much easier to decipher than are links embedded in long paragraphs of text.

Fig. 5.2
Here's how my list
of information
appears in Internet
Explorer.

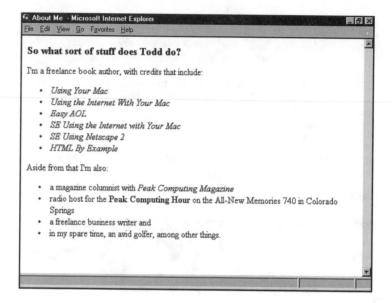

Simplify Large Amounts of Information

Whenever you have several items of related information, you should consider using a list to make it readable. For example, let's say I was creating a listing of my favorite movies. Rather than typing the names of the movies in paragraph form, creating a list is perfect for this situation.

Each movie is indented and easy to read (see fig. 5.3).

In fact, since HTML lets me choose a numbered list, I could easily turn this into a "top-ten" list by simply changing one tag!

Note

In the last chapter, I showed you how to use the <BR> tag to force the Web browser to display text on the next line. Using the <BR> tag, you can emulate a simple list, although I usually wouldn't recommend it. Lists are indented, bulleted, and can even be numbered, making them much more powerful for displaying separate items than the <BR> tag.

Describe a Step-by-Step Process

Another popular use of lists within Web pages is to describe a specific process one step at a time. HTML automatically numbers each step in ascending order, allowing you to ignore the actual numbering scheme for each step. These types of lists are perfect for creating a training manual.

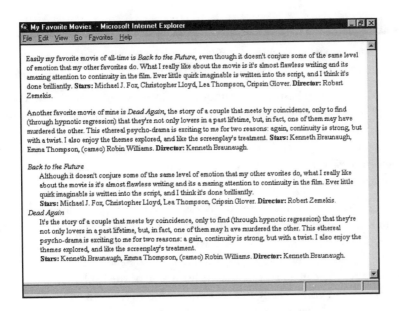

Fig. 5.3
Here are some
of my favorite
movies. Which is
easier to read: the
paragraph or the
list?

II

Creating a Basic Web Page

Whenever you need to outline a process or describe a complicated series of events, I recommend using a list on your Web page. Check out figure 5.4 for a good example of when using a list makes sense.

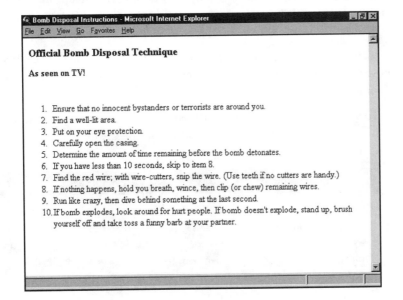

Fig. 5.4
Here's a step-by-
step process that
needs to be
explicit about
the order of
operations.

Add a List to Your Page

Now that you know when you can (and should) use lists, let's take a look at the different types of lists you can add to your Web page.

Lists come in three basic flavors: unordered, ordered, and definition. Although there are others, these are the most commonly used and most widely supported types. Each is similar in that it lists each item on subsequent lines and labels selected text to make information stand out. The main difference between these three list types is how the listed items are numbered and structured.

Adding a list to your page is relatively easy. List tags are containers, so you should start by adding the list opening and closing tags (<UL> and </UL>, <OL> and </OL>, or <DL> and </DL>). Then, with most of these lists, you add a separate tag before the text identifying each item in the list—the list item <LI> tag. Finally, you can add a title for the list inside of the list header tag (<LH> and </LH>) and you're ready to go. Don't get too overwhelmed by all this HTML tagging. I'll step you through HotDog to create them.

Unordered (Bulleted) List

The most common list you will find on Web pages is the unordered list. Each item in an unordered list is identified by a miniature icon preceding it. With a Netscape-compatible browser, you can also display three different icons in front of your list items.

The on and off tags for the unordered list container are <UL> and </UL>. Inside of those tags, you can specify each list item with the <LI> tag. Here's how it works in HotDog:

1. To add an unordered list to your Web page, choose the Insert, List command from HotDog's menu. This brings up the Create List Element dialog box (see fig. 5.5).

   > **Tip**
   >
   > Although you can have as many list items as you want, be careful not to go overboard. A list with too many items is just as unattractive and unreadable as a large paragraph of text. As a general rule of thumb, I try to limit myself to no more than eight items per list. Generally, if I need more items than that, I can divide my list into smaller sublists, which are easier to scan through.

2. From here, you can choose which type of list you want to add and select your desired display options.

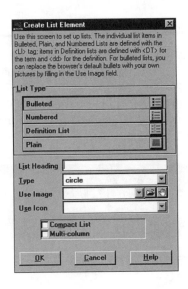

Fig. 5.5
HotDog makes it
easy for you to
add any type of list
you want to your
home page.

3. Then, type your list's title in the List Heading box. The list title appears above your list and serves as a label describing it. (A list heading is not required.)

> **Note**
>
> List headings are not terribly common, and you don't have to use them. If you do, you'll need to edit your document by hand, placing a <BR> after the list heading tags. Non-Netscape browsers seem to have trouble with list headings.

4. After that, choose the type of bulleted icon you want preceding each list item in the Type box—circle, square, or disc.

> **Caution**
>
> Choosing the type of bullet is a Netscape-specific extension. Most other browsers will simply ignore your choice here. Generally the bullet style doesn't matter, unless you're using varying bullet styles to organize your items in some way. That extra information could be lost on some of your users.

The other options—Use Image, Use Icon, Compact List, and Multi-Column—don't really affect how your list appears in most browsers. The first two options are HTML 3.x extensions (which few browsers currently support) and the second two are rarely used with unordered lists, if ever.

Click the OK button and HotDog inserts the necessary HTML code into your document. After the `<LI>` tag you can type the information you want to appear for that list item.

For subsequent list items, type the text, highlight it, and click the Unordered List icon in HotDog's button bar (it looks like bullet points followed by horizontal lines). HotDog inserts the `<LI>` tag for you automatically. Eventually, your list will look like figures 5.6 and 5.7.

Fig. 5.6

Here's my listing of used car models and pricing in HotDog.

The UL icon

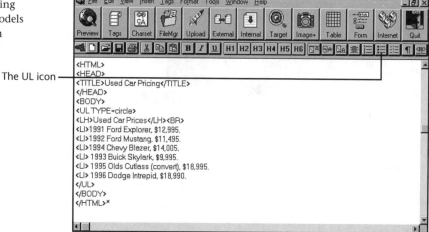

Fig. 5.7

Here's how my list looks when using Internet Explorer to view it.

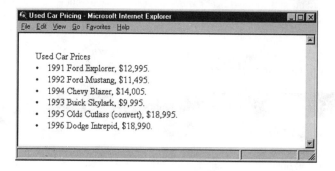

Ordered (Numbered) List

Ordered List works in much the same way as unordered. The only difference between the two list types is that the ordered list adds sequential numbers for each list item instead of bullet points.

The ordered list container uses the `<OL>` and `</OL>` tags. Just like the unordered list, you also use the `<LI>` to identify each element. By default, ordered lists number each element, beginning with one.

I use ordered lists to describe information that I want ranked in order (think of Letterman's Top Ten List—he uses an ordered list), or to describe each step in a process that must be followed in order.

Adding an ordered list to your Web page with HotDog is just as easy as adding an unordered one. Follow these steps:

1. Choose Insert, List from HotDog's menu. The Create List Element dialog box appears.

2. Choose Numbered from the List Type box.

3. In the drop-down Type menu, choose the way in which you want to label each of your list elements. The default is numerical values (1, 2, 3, etc.). You can choose between numbers, letters, and Roman numerals.

4. Once you've chosen how to number your list items, you can pick which number at which your list will begin counting. The default is 1. Type a number in the First Number box to create a list beginning with a different value.

> **Caution**
>
> Once again, realize that only Netscape-compatible browsers will add special numbers and letters, or allow you to start with a value other than 1. Using these Netscape extensions will make your list look very different to users of other, incompatible browsers.

5. Click the OK button to create the HTML required.

Just like the unordered list, you can add as many `<LI>` elements as you want to your list of items. Figure 5.8 shows a simple unordered list in HotDog and figure 5.9 shows it in Internet Explorer after clicking the Preview button.

Fig. 5.8
Here's my listing
for my travel
itinerary.

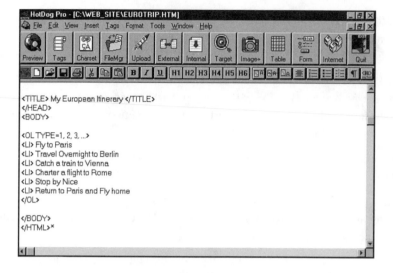

Fig. 5.9
The Netscape view
of my European
trip itinerary, in
order of my visits.

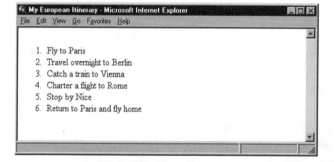

Tip

Use the ordered list icon (it looks like a list of numbers with horizontal lines following each) from the HotDog button bar to easily mark text as additional items in your list.

Definition Lists

Definition lists work slightly differently than other types of lists. Instead of having a single <LI> tag for each element, the definition list requires two tags. The <DT> (definition term) tag is used to identify text listed as a separate element, usually the term to be defined. The <DD> (definition) tag places the following information indented and below the <DT> text. One look at a definition list and you'll immediately understand where it gets its name.

Add a definition list just like the other two lists, except choose Definition List in the Create List Element dialog box.

Of course, a dictionary is an ideal use for a definition list. You can list each term and its definition easily in HTML. However, you'll soon find many other uses for a definition list on your Web page. Anything that could use both a "title" or "term" and a separate description is ideal for a definition list.

Earlier in this chapter, I used a definition list for my favorite movies. Here's how that works in HotDog (see fig. 5.10). Look at figure 5.11 to see how Internet Explorer displays my definition list.

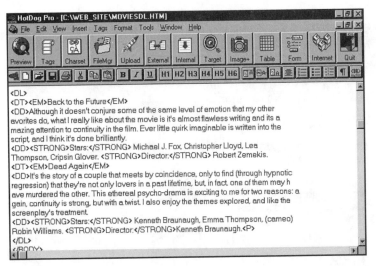

Fig. 5.10
Here's my definiton listing of favorite movies.

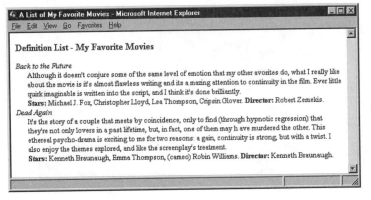

Fig. 5.11
My movies list is easy to read and logically organized.

Lists within Lists

One nice feature of lists is the ability to *nest* them inside each other. Creating lists within lists allows you to have several levels of organized material. You can embed several levels of lists on your page.

Adding a list within a list is the same process as creating a single list. There are no special HTML tags—just the list tags you've already learned. In essence, you simply replace one of the <LI> items with an entire list. Make sure you use the closing tag for each sublist, </UL>, to keep the user's browser from getting confused. You can even embed different types of lists within each other.

> **Tip**
>
> When you add lists inside of lists, line up each level of the list with tabs when you are creating your Web page. Although the tabs won't show up when viewed by a browser, lists are much easier to maintain in HotDog if they are organized well.

Here's an example of adding several sublists within a larger one (see figs. 5.12 and 5.13).

Fig. 5.12
Here's how HotDog shows a bunch of lists bundled into a large one.

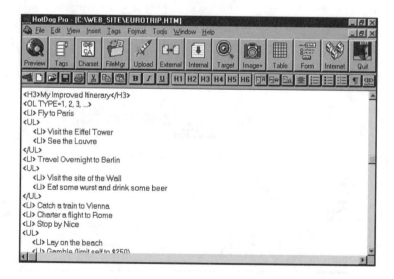

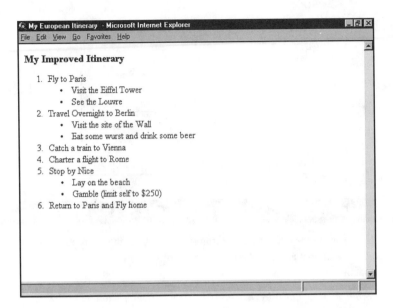

Fig. 5.13
My European itinerary is starting to get in shape.

Tabling Your Home Page

The one drawback of using lists is that they are one-dimensional objects. This means that you can only organize information on subsequent lines. Tables, on the other hand, allow you to line up data in organized rows and columns. You get the flexibility of having two dimensions to display information on your home page.

It's important to understand that there are appropriate times to use tables, so they don't waste space on your Web page. I tend to use tables to compare and contrast similar pieces of information because you can use several different columns and rows. Each row and column can be labeled, allowing you to emulate a spreadsheet-type appearance.

A good table can make your page look very neat and organized and offer a lot of information to the viewer at the same time. A bad, or inappropriate, table splits up your page and makes the point you are trying to convey confusing. Figure 5.14 shows a sample table.

Fig. 5.14
Here's a table
that may come in
handy for baseball
fans.

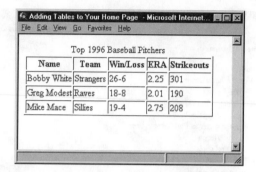

Caution

Tables are one of the major Netscape-compatible features that I talk about in this book. Be aware that anyone who uses a browser that doesn't support Netscape-compatible tags will see a bunch of jumbled text.

Since virtually everyone uses Netscape or Internet Explorer—and new browsers are supporting tables—I wouldn't lose too much sleep over this. But, you should be aware of the problem.

Add a Table

Adding tables to your home page can be complicated because several different tags are used. You start with the <TABLE> container tags and several other tags that define how information should appear. Table 5.1 gives a complete description of table tags.

Table 5.1 HTML Table Tags

Tag	Description
<TABLE> and </TABLE>	This surrounds the entire table. This tag tells the browser to expect the other table tags listed in this table. Add the BORDER attribute (<TABLE BORDER> and </TABLE>) to this tag if you want a grid to appear, separating each row and column with a thin line.
<CAPTION> and </CAPTION>	Text within these tags serves as the tables' explanatory caption.
<TH> and </TH>	This slightly enlarges and bolds text to serve as row and column headers.
<TR> and </TR>	This identifies each row in the table. This tag isn't critical, but makes your HTML code more complete.

Tag	Description
<TD> and </TD>	The text that should go into each cell in the table is surrounded by these tags.

Adding all those tags up makes it confusing to create a multi-row table if you're not careful. Remember that simple table for baseball fans? Figure 5.15 shows the HTML that was used to create it. You can't see it all because it's so long.

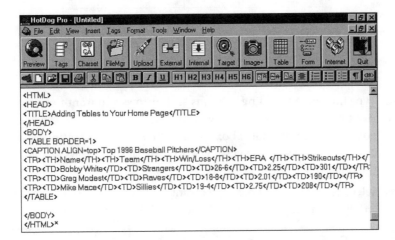

Fig. 5.15
There's a lot of HTML for even a small table.

Whew, all that just for a little table. Fortunately for us, a nice automatic table creator is built into HotDog. Once you get the hang of using HotDog, you'll be able to add new tables easily. You'll also learn the HTML specifics so you can modify and create great-looking tables.

Follow these steps to add a simple table to your home page:

1. Click the Table icon to bring up the Create Table dialog box (see fig. 5.16).

2. To create the same table above, type **Top 1996 Baseball Pitchers** in the Caption text box. You can choose to display the caption above or below the table. Unless your table is exceedingly small, leave the caption above it so viewers can look at the caption first.

3. In the Columns and Rows text boxes, type the number of each you would like in your table. Rows and columns that you want to use as labels should be included in this count. For this table example, type **4** in the Rows box and **5** in the Columns box. HotDog creates the table for you in the box labeled Sample Table.

Fig. 5.16
Here's my table,
all ready to be
created.

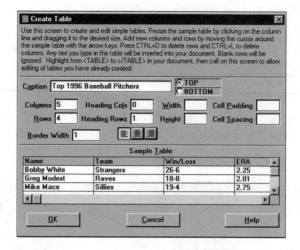

4. Type how many heading columns and/or rows you want to have in the Heading Cols and Heading Rows boxes. HotDog shades in the heading boxes in the sample table box to make them easy to identify. Let's use only a single heading row; so type **1** in the Heading Rows box and leave the other one (Heading Cols) blank.

5. Select how thick of a border you want for your table. For this example, let's go for a simple border and put **1** in the Border Width box.

> **Note**
>
> Here's a rundown of the other boxes in the Create Table dialog box: Width and Height let you force the table to a certain size (in pixels); Cell Padding and Cell Spacing let you add spaces between your tables, rows, and columns; and Alignment buttons allow you to set where in each cell your text is aligned (left, right, or centered).

6. Now type your information in each box listed in the Sample Table. The shaded gray boxes are the table headers and the white boxes represent each table cell. Use your mouse, arrow, and tab keys to maneuver around the Sample Table.

7. When you're finished, click the OK button and HotDog creates all the HTML code for you.

Tip

It's a good idea to take some time and format your table tags and text to be easily read in HotDog, in case you want to make changes later. Trying to update your tables is much simpler when it is readable. I space my tables out to make them readable using tabs and carriage returns.

Using Advanced Table Features

Now that you can create a good-looking, simple table, let's try adding a little flavor to it. Netscape extensions offer several impressive ways to customize your tables.

I'm not going to go into excruciating detail for each of these options because you have to type them in yourself (HotDog doesn't support them, yet), and they can be overwhelming. I'll explain each one and give you an example of how they can help you organize your home page tables.

Lines Spanning Multiple Rows

As you start using tables more and more often, you'll occasionally find situations where you wish your information could span multiple rows. That's where the ROWSPAN attribute comes into use.

ROWSPAN is a special keyword that you add to the <TD> tag for a specific cell. To have a cell span two rows instead of the default one, try using <TD ROWSPAN=2>Your extended Text HERE</TD> instead of <TD>Your Text Here</TD>.

When your table displays, you'll now be taking up two rows for the cell you added ROWSPAN to. Here's how I used ROWSPAN to change my baseball table:

```
<TR>
<TD>Bobby White</TD>
<TD ROWSPAN=2>Strangers</TD>
<TD>26-6</TD>
<TD>2.25</TD>
<TD>301</TD>
</TR>
<TR>
<TD>Kevin Toast</TD>
<TD>12-6</TD>
<TD>4.98</TD>
<TD>278</TD>
</TR>
```

Figure 5.17 shows the changed table in Internet Explorer.

II

Creating a Basic Web Page

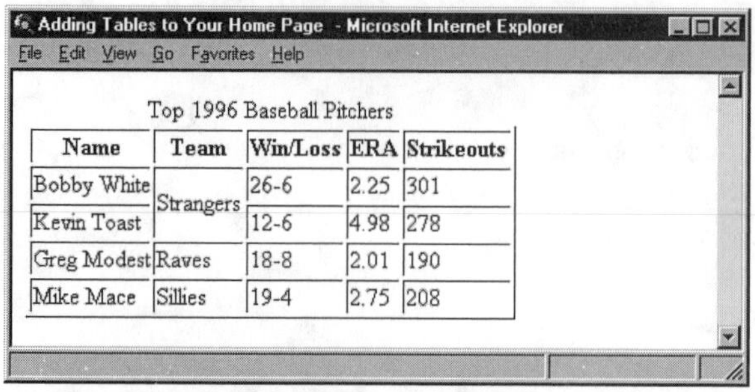

Fig. 5.17
Here's how
ROWSPAN could
shape up your
table.

Top 1996 Baseball Pitchers				
Name	Team	Win/Loss	ERA	Strikeouts
Bobby White	Strangers	26-6	2.25	301
Kevin Toast		12-6	4.98	278
Greg Modest	Raves	18-8	2.01	190
Mike Mace	Sillies	19-4	2.75	208

Caution

When you use ROWSPAN (or COLSPAN, described next), make sure you take into account the reduced number of rows or columns you need to fill for other table entries. In the table I created for figure 5.17, I used five <TD> data elements for Bobby White, but I only used four <TD> data elements for Kevin Toast. That's because the Strangers entry is going to span two rows, filling in that fifth cell for Kevin.

Spanning Multiple Columns

As with ROWSPAN, you can also have specific cells span multiple columns. Using the built-in keyword COLSPAN, you can instruct your table to span across as many cells as you want.

Use COLSPAN just like you did ROWSPAN, as in the following example:

```
<TR>
<TH COLSPAN=2>Personal Information</TH>
<TH COLSPAN=3>Statistics</TH>
</TR>
<TR>
<TH>Name</TH>
<TH>Team</TH>
<TH>Win/Loss record</TH>
<TH>ERA</TH>
<TH>Strikeouts</TH>
</TR>
```

Look at figure 5.18 to see my COLSPAN in action.

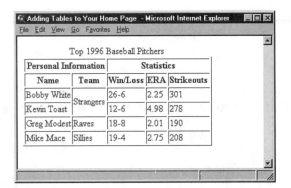

Fig. 5.18
You can use
ROWSPAN and
COLSPAN in the
<TH> tags.

Embedding Lists in Tables

Tables can be treated just like any other HTML element and be broken down into lists as described earlier in this chapter. All three list types perform the same when embedded within a table. Make sure you carefully add the closing tags when you add a list to your table—they're easy to forget.

In figure 5.19, I've added a simple unordered list to my baseball table.

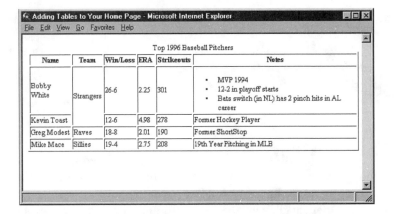

Fig. 5.19
Lists inside of tables look really slick, don't you think?

Note

If you really are looking for a challenge, try embedding a table within a table. The effects are neat, but keeping track of your HTML can be a pain! You've got to make sure you use all of the closing tags properly (</TABLE>), and lining up each element is difficult. Embedded tables often don't need a header or a border.

Setting Your Text Alignment

HTML 3.2 extensions to HTML tables also let you customize the alignment of each cell, both vertically and horizontally. With a special attribute, ALIGN, these settings offer you increased flexibility over how your table looks. HotDog lets you set horizontal alignment for your entire table in the Create Table Dialog box (but not your vertical alignment setting).

The ALIGN keyword can have three settings and is used in the same spot as the spanning keywords above—within the <TD> tag. (These alignment tags can also be used with other table tags, including the <TABLE> tag itself and the <TR> tag.) Use Table 5.2 to understand the use of these two keywords.

Table 5.2   Alignment Attribute Descriptions

Attribute Setting	Description
ALIGN=LEFT	Left justifies text in the cell
ALIGN=CENTER	Centers the text horizontally within the cell
ALIGN=RIGHT	Right justifies text in the cell

Tip

Several Web pages use the ALIGN attribute to organize graphics within a table. By removing the table's border, you can perfectly line up sets of graphics in an organized fashion. It works great with money decimals, too.

Table Alternatives

If you are concerned that non-Netscape-compatible browsers (like the older AOL browser) can't display tables, find them too bulky to use, or would prefer to not use them at all, you'll be pleased to find that there are a few popular options to using tables.

The two most popular options are using extra lists, or the <PRE> and </PRE> HTML tags. These two workarounds offer table-like functionality but are limited in nature.

Lists Can Replace Tables

Even though lists are one-dimensional displays of information, if properly used, you can replace virtually any table with a couple of lists.

Take the baseball player table that I've been using. I could replace that table with a few lists (see fig. 5.20). Of course, it's not as easy to read as a table, and makes the user scroll through the screen.

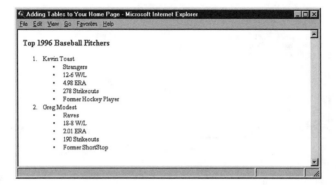

Fig. 5.20
Although they present the same amount of information, lists aren't as flexible as tables.

Preformatted Text

In Chapter 4, I talked about the <PRE> and </PRE> tags which display information as you actually type it on your home page, without any browser interpretations on how it should be presented.

You can use these tags to emulate a table as well. It's not as flashy, and you can't have graphical borders, but most people won't even notice the difference. Using carriage returns, spaces, and tabs, I've created the following table as preformatted text (see fig. 5.21):

```
<PRE>
Name            Team        W/L     ERA       Strikeouts
Bobby White     Strangers   26-6    2.25      225
Kevin Toast     Strangers   16-6    4.98      278
Greg Modest     Raves       18-8    2.01      190
</PRE>
```

Tip

It's easiest to align this data if you use a monospaced font, like Courier. To change the font in HotDog, choose Tools, Options, and the Editing tab.

Note

You can even use text formatting tags (like <EM> and <STRONG>) within your pre-formatted text to italicize or bold, respectively, different parts of your table. Realize, though, that anything other than plain text will probably not align properly in all the various browsers—even if it looks right to you when you test it in Internet Explorer.

Fig. 5.21
The <PRE> tag lets
me replace this
simple table with
no problems.

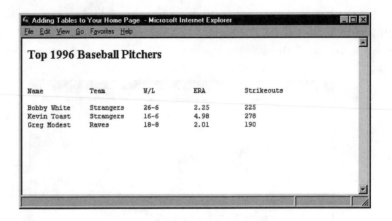

CHAPTER 6

Spicing Up Your Web Pages with Graphics

You're already halfway through this book, and you've got a decent looking home page to prove it. So far, I've shown you how to plan and produce a good-looking Web page that isn't too complicated to update.

Now that you're familiar with lists, tables, and text formatting features, you can organize your page however you like. But text formatting isn't the real reason the WWW is so popular—it's the ability to add cool graphics and pictures to your page alongside your text that gets people's attention.

As you've probably already noticed, almost every page on the WWW uses graphics or pictures to enhance its site and make it more enjoyable to visit. This chapter teaches you how to spice up your home page with vivid graphics, colorful backgrounds, and useful icons. You probably won't even recognize your home page after you're finished with this chapter!

Pros and Cons of Web Page Graphics

Images and graphics are vital to the Web's existence. The WWW is the only Internet tool that lets you look at images and text on the same screen at the same time. Imagine picking up an issue of *Newsweek* that had no pictures in it. It would probably be pretty boring, no matter how they formatted their text. Looking at a Web page without any graphics is like reading a coffee table book that has no pictures. It just doesn't make much sense.

You'll learn how you can easily add images and pictures to your home page to make it more attractive and fun to browse. See figure 6.1 for a prime example of a Web site that takes advantage of graphics.

Fig. 6.1
Can you just imagine a page discussing Michelangelo (**http:// www.emf.net/ wm/paint/ auth/ michelangelo/**) without pictures?

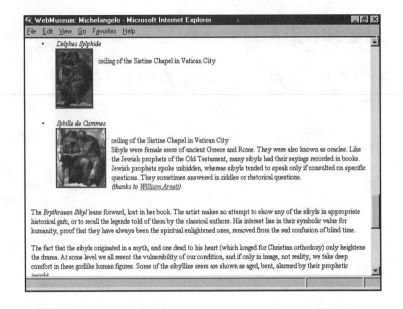

Then again, a site doesn't have to be completely about graphics. One of the keys to Web page design, in fact, is making it compelling and graphical without forcing your user to wait many minutes to download the page. And that's quite a trick. An example of a page that does a good job of this is Yahoo's home page (see fig. 6.2). Notice that it appears very graphical and professionally-designed. In fact, it's using very few images.

Even a few, well-placed graphics can add some serious zip to your pages.

Fig. 6.2
Yahoo (**http:// www.yahoo.com**) is one of the most used and best known spots on the WWW.

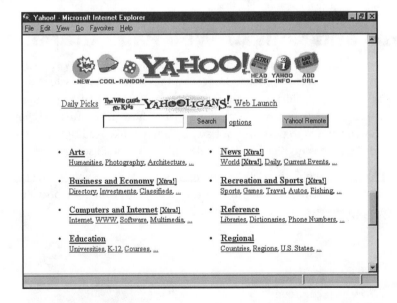

You've also got to be careful not to overdo your home page with too many images. Before you read this chapter and decide to add 100 plus images to your one Web page (or even, seriously, more than 5–10), remember that it's easy to go overboard. With too many icons and images lining your home page, your text will get lost in the shuffle, visitors won't understand what they're looking at, and all your efforts for a great looking home page could be for naught.

Where You Can Find Graphics, Images, and Pictures

Now that you're convinced you need to add an image or two to your Web page, where do you find them? Acquiring images can be the most difficult part of the entire process. Whether you want a simple icon or a panoramic view of the Grand Canyon, it's hard to find that perfect image to stick on your page.

Realizing this, I've included hundreds of different images, icons, and backgrounds on the CD-ROM in the back of this book. You have animals, famous people, neat icons, and radiant backgrounds directly at your fingertips. And if these don't fit your needs, I've also included some tips on how you can get your own images for your home page.

On the CD

On the Enclosed CD-ROM

When we were putting together the enclosed CD-ROM, we asked ourselves this question: "What kind of stuff would people find useful on a CD-ROM in this book?" The first answer that jumped to my mind was graphics. I'm talking about images, icons, pictures, drawings, sketches, and lots more! This CD is your main resource when creating your own home page, and I've included all the appropriate material.

I've organized the images on the CD-ROM into three main categories:

- **Pictures**—You can find shots of animals, famous people, and lots of other images that should look familiar. This is a generic set of pictures that you may be able to use on your home page.

- **Icons**—Icons are used to represent information in a familiar and graphical way. On the CD, you can find construction icons, home icons, navigation icons, and even spiffy looking lines that can replace the <HR> tag!

- **Backgrounds**—Covered later this chapter, HTML 3.2 extensions allow you to place an image behind your text so it appears as a background. This image gives your home page some flair and makes it much more colorful. Several hundred sample backgrounds are on the CD so you have plenty of choices.

Create Your Own Images

While you'll probably find lots of useful and nice images on the CD-ROM, you're also likely to want to put a few of your own customized pictures on your home page. You may want to show yourself, your family, or even a pet.

To put your images on your home page, you'll need to scan them into graphic files. Scanning is the process of digitizing an existing picture so it can be displayed on your PC. You can scan photographs, drawings, and logos to be added to your home page easily. AOL members have two different options here.

Scanning Images Yourself

To scan pictures yourself, you'll need a separate piece of computer equipment called—believe it or not—a *scanner*. Scanners range in price from $79 (black-and-white) to $999 (high-end color scanner) and are sold in most computer stores. If you intend to put a lot of images on your home page, purchasing a scanner may be a worthwhile investment.

> **Tip**
>
> For my home page, I didn't buy a scanner. Instead, I went down to my local copying store and rented their high-quality scanner for an hour or two. I paid about $25 and I got everything scanned and taken care of in one step.

The PicturePlace (PictureWeb) Service

On America Online, you can access a special service designed for scanning your personal images into electronic files for use on your home page. It's called PicturePlace (keyword **PicturePlace** or **PictureWeb**), and, at least currently, it offers your first two scans free of charge (see fig. 6.3).

Here's the basic drill. All you have to do is send the snapshot you want to use on your Web site through U.S. mail to PictureWeb. It'll scan them into electronic graphics files and place them on its Web site. From there, you can download them to your PC for use on your home page.

Tip

You can access the PictureWeb site from any browser, whether or not you use AOL for access. The URL **http://www.pictureweb.com/** can be used to go directly to PictureWeb.

Fig. 6.3
The PicturePlace area on AOL will scan your snapshots for use on the Web. (Click the 3 button to go the PictureWeb URL with AOL's browser.)

Borrow Images from Other Pages

Another common way of obtaining images for your home page is to "borrow" them from other pages that you've visited. Built into most Web browsers is the ability save any image you see into a separate file with just a few mouse clicks.

Here's how to save an image that you're looking at in Internet Explorer for Windows. The following steps show you how to borrow an image from my home page (this same procedure works on any and every Web site you visit):

1. Go to **http://members.aol.com/tstauffer/** and find a good image (like one of the book jackets or one of the logos—you can't really want a picture of me). When viewing a page, move your cursor over the image you want to save separately on your computer.

2. Click the right mouse button on a picture to bring up several Internet Explorer options (see fig. 6.4).

Fig. 6.4
Internet Explorer
doesn't do much
for copyright laws,
does it?

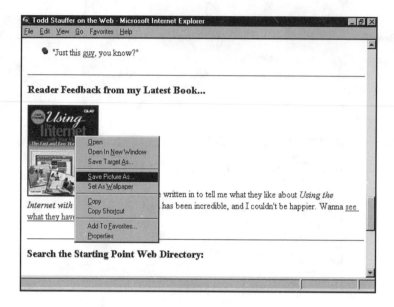

3. Choose Save Picture As from the list of options to bring up the Save As
   dialog box (see fig. 6.5).

Fig. 6.5
Once you click
Save, the image is
yours forever.

4. Internet Explorer fills in the default filename automatically (you can
   change it if you want). Choose where on your hard drive you want to
   save the image and then click the Save button.

> **Caution**
>
> Be aware that many images you might see when browsing on the WWW are pro-
> tected under copyright laws. Even though you can save images with Internet Ex-
> plorer, you must have permission to use borrowed images on your own home page.
> You have permission to use all the images found on the CD included in this book.

AOL's Personal Publisher Images

One way to quickly add some professional-looking graphics to your Web pages is to use the images provided in the Personal Publisher Images area. This is basically a bunch of graphics you can choose to download to your PC and then use on your page. Eventually, you'll upload them back to AOL in the My Place area.

Here's how to get the graphics:

1. Start from the Personal Publisher screen (keyword **Personal Publisher**). Click the Images for Your Home Page button.

2. In the Home Page Graphics dialog box, click the Graphics Available For Use In Your Home Page button. You'll see a download library of files (see fig. 6.6).

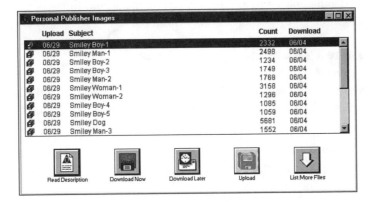

Fig. 6.6
Picking and choosing graphics for your home page.

3. Scroll through the list until you see something you think might be interesting. (You can click the List More Files button to see more images.) When you see a promising name, double-click the filename.

4. Now you'll be in the description window for this image. You'll see a thumbnail of the graphic and a quick write-up. If you like it, click either Download Now or Download Later at the bottom of the screen. From here, it's just a typical AOL download. By default, the graphics will appear in the DOWNLOAD subdirectory of the AOL directory on your hard drive.

To be frank, there isn't an amazing amount of images here. Another interesting place to look on the AOL service might be the PC Graphic Arts & Animation Forum (keyword **PGR**).

> **Caution**
>
> If you download graphics from the forum, make sure they're "public domain" or that you otherwise have the creator's permission before putting them on your Web pages.

Adding an Image to Your Web Page

Now that you know where to get images from, let's start adding them to your home page. This section uses HotDog to add images to your home page and teaches you how to use the various HTML options when adding images.

I will explain what you need to understand about images and their file types. Then, I'll describe how to add a simple image to your home page. I'm also going to give some image tips and tricks that will make your home page easier to use and more enjoyable for visitors who stop by.

Using the Proper Image File Types

There are several different formats that images can be saved in. These formats each have their own advantages and disadvantages for usage. On the WWW, two main image formats are most commonly supported: GIF and JPEG.

The GIF (Graphical Interchange Format) file type was pioneered by CompuServe (the Information Service) to provide information in a standard graphical format. GIF set an image standard years ago and was the first file type supported by the WWW.

Recently, a newer image format, labeled JPEG (Joint Photographic Experts Group) was developed and has proven to be significantly more efficient than GIFs in several circumstances, especially with larger images. This means that JPEG files tend to be smaller and consequently download quicker when browsing the WWW. JPEG uses a special image compression technique that makes it better for pictures and snapshots. It handles colors and detail better than the GIF format.

The only drawback to the JPEG standard for graphics is that the compression scheme (which makes files smaller) is a little bit more *lossy* than GIF files. Basically, that means that some of the information is lost in the translation, and some JPEGs, especially at smaller sizes and using fewer colors, will look a bit less crisp than the original.

Internet Explorer supports both GIF and JPEG file types. Personally, I use GIF for most of my images because most of them are rather small and use few colors (like text logos and background). In this book, we'll talk about using both types of images. Not all browsers support JPEG, although most of the newer ones do.

For your convenience, I've included a program on the CD-ROM so you can switch images from one format to another easily. Use Paint Shop Pro to convert any images between various graphics formats such as GIF to JPEG or vice versa.

On the CD

Adding the Image

This example should look familiar to you. I'm using the Mountain Flying Club home page to show you how adding graphics can make quite a difference. We'll build a special page to show off one of the club's planes. See figure 6.7 for a plain text-only page.

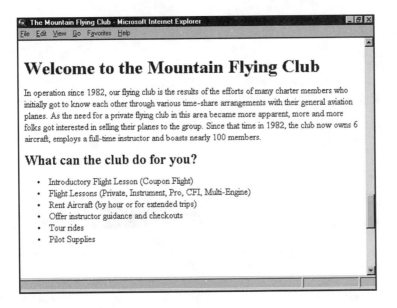

Fig. 6.7
Here's the initial boring flying club page.

Adding images with HotDog is pretty easy. Simply put your cursor at the spot where you want to place the image and click the Image Icon to bring up the Image Properties dialog box (see fig. 6.8). For my plane description page, I'm going to add the image to the top of my page, right above my <H1> </H1> header. You can place images anywhere on your home page between the <BODY> and </BODY> tags.

Images are defined in HTML with the <IMG SRC=> tag. So, to insert a GIF file named PLANE1.GIF on a Web page, HotDog adds the following line of HTML:

```
<IMG SRC="PLANE1.GIF">
```

II

Creating a Basic Web Page

Fig. 6.8
Type the image's
filename that you
want to add to
your home page.

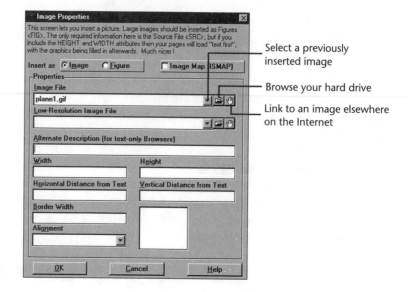

Select a previously
inserted image

Browse your hard drive

Link to an image elsewhere
on the Internet

That tag tells the browser to display an image whose source filename is
PLANE1.GIF. When you view this page, the image will appear integrated along
with your text.

Type the full file and path name of the image (that is, the file and path name
it will have in your My Place directory) in the image file box. On the right of
the box are three icons (explained in Table 6.1) that may help you create the
path and filename of your image.

Table 6.1   Image File Icon Table

To...	...Do This
Select a previously inserted image	HotDog keeps track of the last few images you've added to your home page.
Click images	Click the icon to bring up a list of images inserted recently.
Browse your hard drive	Built into HotDog is a mini file manager. Click this icon to browse through the files on your hard drive and add images to your home page by selecting them.
Link to an image elsewhere	You can also link directly to an image on the Internet at a different spot on the WWW. Clicking this button brings up a separate dialog box where you can build the URL. I talk more about linking in the next chapter.

Use the icons or type in your image's filename yourself. I'll type in PLANE1.GIF to add a Cessna image to my page; click OK to add the proper HTML tags to your page.

Figure 6.9 shows the same page shown in figure 6.8, with the PLANE1.GIF image added to it.

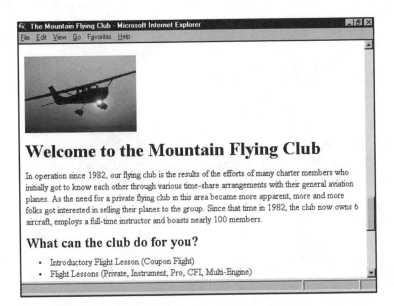

Fig. 6.9
Just one image makes a page instantly more attractive!

II

Creating a Basic Web Page

Note

Linking correctly to your images requires that you understand how to point to files that are in a different file directory or even on a different drive.

For example, if your image (PLANE1.GIF) is located in the exact same directory as the HTML file, you don't have to worry about pointing to other directories and drives. Your HTML tag is:

```
<IMG SRC="PLANE1.GIF">
```

But eventually, your home page images and HTML text may not be located in the same directory. If your images are located in a separate subdirectory named IMAGES, then your tag would be:

```
<IMG SRC="IMAGES/PLANE1.GIF">
```

(continues)

(continued)

If your images are located in a directory one level above your current subdirectory in your hard drive structure, then you would use this tag:

```
<IMG SRC="../PLANE.GIF">
```

Any combination of the previous tags can be used to tell the user's browser where to look for your images when trying to display your page.

Image File Size Guidelines

One of the most important things you should think about when it comes to using images on your Web pages is the file *size*. Whenever someone visits your home page, they must download all the text and images to their PC. Although text doesn't take very long to download, images can take awhile, so you want to be aware of how large your images are and how long you're making your users wait before they can view your page.

It may not seem important to you, but consider the time you've spent surfing the Web. Ever get annoyed when you're waiting for a page to show up? Often that's because the browser is waiting for images to be completely downloaded to your PC. Until that happens, it may not be able to release control to you so that you can scroll through the page.

Consider that the typical TV commercial is 30 seconds long. If you've got a page that takes twice that long to download, it might cause your user to just move on to the next page. Every page takes a little while on the Web, but one of the secrets to getting people to visit your site is to make it as responsive as possible. Dedicated Web surfers are spending a lot of time watching graphics download to their computer. If you help them out a bit, they'll be much more likely to revisit your site.

Tip

If you scan your own images, realize that graphics for Web pages generally don't need to be scanned at anything over 100 dpi. This keeps file size as small as possible, while still offering good enough quality for typical computer monitors.

Maximum File Size

As a general rule of thumb, I try to limit any image on my Web pages to 20 kilobytes (KB). With a 20 KB limit, your images can be of sufficient detail, yet not make visitors chew off their fingernails waiting for the page to download.

Actually, I use 20 KB as a very rough guideline. In the next section when I talk about icons, you'll find that most of them are extremely small (2–6 KB) and download quickly. Occasionally, you might have a fantastic image that is larger than 20K. Don't worry too much about using it; just be aware that if you add too many larger images, they add up quickly.

> **Tip**
>
> It's also a good idea to keep track of your entire home page's file size. Add up the size of your HTML file and the file size of each image you use. Your total should rest below 100 KB, preferably between 30–60 KB. And, if you have more than one page on your home site, you should try to make the other pages even smaller. With a 14.4 baud modem, visitors who stop by will spend 1–2 minutes downloading 100 KB before they can enjoy the full glory of your page. That's a long time to wait.

Resizing and Thumbnailing Your Images

If all the images you like are larger, you have several other options for including them on your home page without making each visitor download them. You can resize most of your images, making them smaller on-screen and decreasing their actual file size, as well.

Several professional packages, such as Adobe Photoshop, allow you to manipulate image sizes. Included on the CD, you'll find several shareware tools that will let you resize your images. Although not nearly as robust as Photoshop, they're much cheaper and can accomplish most of what you need for your pages. I use Paint Shop Pro or WinJPG to resize and create thumbnails of all my graphics.

Resizing makes your image smaller, and sometimes harder to see. Some images look fine when shrunk; others become barely viewable. I've had great success resizing my images. One image I used was originally the size of the entire screen and took up 190K (a long download for that single image). After resizing it to about one-fourth the screen size, the picture is down to about 43K, a reasonable size for my home page (although still a bit large).

Another option, related to resizing your images, is creating thumbnail images. Thumbnail images are miniature duplicates of larger images. You could create a small thumbnail of a large image on your home page, and include a link to the full-size image that visitors can see if they want. (Read "Using Images as Links" in Chapter 7 for more information on how to do this.)

Thumbnails are extremely popular because they let visitors pick and choose which full size images they want from a list of miniature ones (see fig. 6.10).

Fig. 6.10
Using thumbnails, the Mountain Flying Club can let users pick and choose which planes to view.

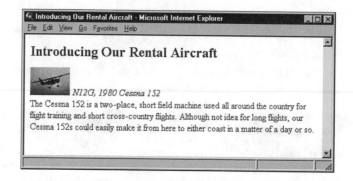

> **Tip**
>
> If your images are all in GIF format, try converting them into JPEG format. You might notice a four-to-one file size difference from GIF to JPEG for certain images!

Manipulating Your Web Page Images

With images added, you'll notice a big difference in the attractiveness of your home page. However, there are several other HTML options which will help you manipulate and organize images. One of the most important of these lets you provide alternative text for visitors to read if they can't view your images for some reason.

Several of these HTML options will only work with Netscape-compatible browsers, but they're often worth using. You can set image alignment, flow text around images, and size your images manually on your home page. I'll show you how to set these options with HotDog, and then explain them individually.

Using HotDog to Set Image Options

Earlier in this chapter, you saw how to use HotDog to add a simple image to your HTML document. There is also a second HotDog command that allows you to choose your advanced image placement characteristics from different menus.

To bring up the advanced image placing tools, choose Insert, Image (Advanced) from the HotDog menu to bring up the Image Properties dialog box (see fig. 6.11).

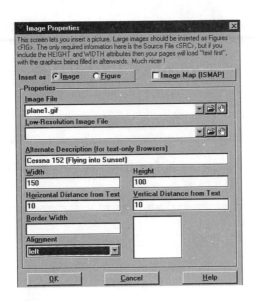

Fig. 6.11
I can add my
image and set all
the options in one
step with this
dialog box.

Here's a quick run-down of the different options available to you from this
screen (see Table 6.2). Read the following sections to understand these
options thoroughly and see examples on using them.

Table 6.2   Available Options on the HotDog Screen

Option	Action
Image File	Enter the filename and path to your image.
Low-Resolution Image File	Choose an image that is less detailed to appear first before your regular image is displayed. Rarely used unless you have gigantic images on your page.
Alternate Description	Enter the text that appears in the ALT attribute.
Width	Enter a number in pixels to indicate how wide your image is (WIDTH attribute). Some browsers use this information to format pages more quickly.
Height	Enter a number in pixels for your picture's height (HEIGHT attribute).
Horizontal Distance from Text	Add horizontal white space (in pixels) between your text and images.
Vertical Distance from Text	Add vertical white space (in pixels) between your text and images.

(continues)

Table 6.2 Continued	
Option	**Action**
Border Width	Create a black border around your image. Useful in framing your images.
Alignment	Choose values allowed with the ALIGN keyword.

Choose your settings and click the OK button. HotDog will add the HTML tag and all your settings for you.

> **Note**
>
> HotDog is only useful for setting your image options when you first add the image to your home page. To make changes after that, you've got to manually edit your HTML. The following sections explain the required HTML to set each option.

Providing Alternative Text

Some browsers don't support both GIF and JPEG, while others don't support any images at all. Although Internet Explorer supports both of these popular image types, you can tell it not to load any images when browsing WWW pages so you don't have to spend lots of time downloading them.

> **Tip**
>
> To keep Internet Explorer from downloading images, choose View, Options to bring up the Options dialog box. Make sure the General tab is selected, and then click the checkbox marked Pictures. When checked, pictures are automatically downloaded; when unchecked, the ALT text is shown instead.

To accommodate these situations, it is a common courtesy to always provide alternative text descriptions to the images you include on your home page. Alternative text is part of the <IMG> tag. You add the ALT= attribute to your tag and type text inside the quotation marks. If I add alternative text to my previous PLANE1.GIF example, my new tag looks like the following:

```
<IMG SRC="PLANE1.GIF" ALT="1980 Cessna 172">
```

If I turn off image loading in Internet Explorer, or view the page with a browser that doesn't recognize GIF files, people will see 1980 Cessna 172 where the image should appear. Figure 6.12 shows how alternative text appears on WWW pages.

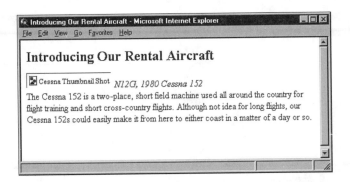

Fig. 6.12
Here's how images
are displayed when
Internet Explorer
users choose not to
load them.

Tip

You can add alternate text with the Image Properties dialog box (choose Insert,
Image from the HotDog menu). Type in alternate text below your image's filename.

Aligning Your Image

When you place images on your home page, you have several different options for how they align themselves on the screen with respect to text on
your page. Netscape-compatible browsers recognize the ALIGN attribute as part
of the <IMG> tag.

With ALIGN, you have control over where the image is placed on screen and
how text appears around it. You have eight different ALIGN options, as listed
in Table 6.3.

Table 6.3   Image Alignment Table

Option	Action
LEFT	Lines the image up on the left side of the page; multiple lines of text wrap around the side of the image on the right.
RIGHT	Lines the image up on the right side of the page; multiple lines of text wrap around the side of the image on the left.
TOP	Aligns the image to the tallest item on the line.
TEXTTOP	Aligns the image to the tallest text item on the line (usually appears the exact same as TOP).
MIDDLE	Aligns the bottom of your line of text with the middle of the image.

(continues)

Table 6.3 Continued	
Option	**Action**
ABSMIDDLE	Aligns the middle of your line of text with the middle of the image (very similar to MIDDLE, but used for small images).
BOTTOM	Aligns the bottom of your line of text to the bottom of the image.
BASELINE	Identical to BOTTOM.

Since they're very similar to the other keywords, I wouldn't bother using TEXTTOP, ABSMIDDLE, and BASELINE on your page; they'll just confuse you in the long run.

> **Caution**
>
> Only Netscape-compatible browsers recognize the TEXTTOP, ABSMIDDLE, and BASELINE attribute values for ALIGN. Other browsers often recognize the LEFT, RIGHT, TOP, MIDDLE, and BOTTOM keywords though, since they're part of the HTML 3.x standards.

To set your image's alignment to LEFT, add ALIGN=LEFT to your <IMG> tag. Now, your plane image tag looks like this:

```
<IMG SRC="PLANE1.GIF" ALT="1980 Cessna 172" ALIGN=LEFT>
```

Text on the page wraps to the right of the image, as in figure 6.13.

Fig. 6.13
Using the ALIGN tag lets you control where your image is placed.

> **Note**
>
> When using the LEFT and RIGHT keywords, you might want to also add the Netscape-enhanced <BR> tag to your HTML document. You can add <BR CLEAR=LEFT> and <BR CLEAR=RIGHT> to make sure that text appearing after the image appears below the image instead of next to it.

Sizing Your Image

Besides aligning your image, you can also manually control the height and width of images that appear on your page. Normally, Internet Explorer displays the image at its regular size, but with the HEIGHT and WIDTH attributes you can shrink or enlarge an image's appearance without altering the actual image file.

Defining the image's height and width speeds up page browsing because the browser can save a place for the image on your screen while loading the rest of your home page's text. You must define the HEIGHT and WIDTH of how the image should appear in pixels, thus limiting the size of the picture on-screen.

> **Note**
>
> A pixel (picture element) is a unit of measurement that's used to calculate monitor resolution. To get an idea of how large a pixel is, consider that a standard VGA screen is 640 (Width) by 480 (Height) pixels. Super VGA is 800×600 pixels. Thus, an image that is 320×240 pixels in dimension would take up approximately half a VGA screen.

You can add the HEIGHT and WIDTH keywords to your <IMG> tag the same way you add the alignment and alternative text keywords. Unfortunately, if you've already added the image, you've got to enter these attributes on your page manually, without HotDog's help.

To add HEIGHT and WIDTH attributes to my PLANE1.GIF picture, the HTML code would look like the following:

```
<IMG SRC="PLANE1.GIF" ALT="1980 Cessna 172" ALIGN=LEFT WIDTH=175
HEIGHT=110>
```

The PLANE1.GIF is now set to appear at the pre-defined size of 175 pixels across the screen and 110 pixels tall.

Realize that the HEIGHT and WIDTH attributes, while they can be used for re-sizing graphics, are really designed just for telling browsers what size the graphic is to help it layout and display the page more quickly.

> **Caution**
>
> It's a common mistake, but you shouldn't create thumbnail images with the HEIGHT and WIDTH attributes. Remember that the point of thumbnail images to is make the image's file size smaller for downloading. HEIGHT and WIDTH do not affect the file size of images. Even if the images are displayed smaller on the screen, the entire image must still be downloaded to the user's PC. To create thumbnails, use a special graphics program (like Paint Shop Pro) to make sure you're actually getting the smallest possible image files.

Adding Icons to Your Home Page

Besides adding full color images and pictures to your home page, you can also place all sorts of icons on it as well. While icons technically fall under the term images (they're GIF and JPEG files as well), they are typically extremely small (2–6K) and are used for design, aesthetic, and navigational purposes on Web pages.

Icons come in many shapes and sizes. Ranging from miniature construction icons to colorful lines and buttons, you'll see a wide variety of them on pages across the WWW. Often you won't even realize that you're looking at icons when you browse a home page, because they're so well-integrated into the design.

On the CD

I've included a vast array of icons on the included CD. I can practically guarantee that you'll find several icons that will look great on your home page. I'm going to take you on a brief tour of some of these icons and show you some uses for them on your home page.

Lines and Bars

In Chapter 4, I explained how to use the <HR> tag to separate pieces of your Web page. It's also extremely popular to use simple graphics of lines and bars to replace the <HR> tag.

On the CD

Line graphics exist in all shapes, colors, and designs, and are significantly different than using the <HR> tag. Figure 6.14 gives an example of how I use the file ALUM.GIF (an aluminum bar) instead of the <HR> tag on the flying club home page. You can find this graphic in the /GRAPHICS/ICONS/LINES subdirectory on the attached CD-ROM.

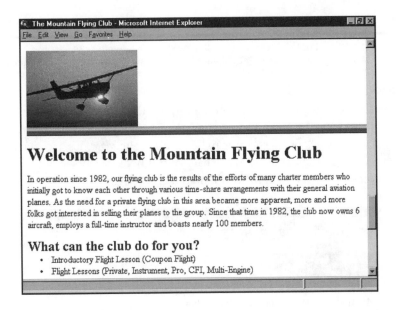

Fig. 6.14
Here's the flying club home page with graphics and a line added.

The page is more attractive, better designed, and fits better with the aviation theme of the page. The following is the HTML code added:

```
<CENTER><IMG SRC="alum.gif"></CENTER>
```

Bullets

Bullets are commonly used to replace the dots that appear when you add an unordered list to your page. You'll find bullets of all sorts of colors and sizes in the /GRAPHICS/ICONS/BULLETS subdirectory on the CD-ROM.

On the CD

When I use bullets, I usually skip using an unordered list in my home page. Instead, I add each list item and then put the <BR> tag after it. The overall effect is a simulated list with neat icons serving as the bullets instead of the unordered list circles and squares.

Tip

Make sure you use the ALIGN keyword when placing bullets on your home page to ensure that your text lines up with the image correctly.

The following is a sample of the HTML code I use to add graphical bullets to the flying club home page:

```
<IMG SRC="bullet.gif" ALIGN=CENTER> Introductory Flight<BR>
<IMG SRC="bullet.gif" ALIGN=CENTER> Flight Lessons<BR>
```

II

Creating a Basic Web Page

```
<IMG SRC="bullet.gif" ALIGN=CENTER> Aircraft Rental<BR>
<IMG SRC="bullet.gif" ALIGN=CENTER> Pilot Supplies<BR>
<IMG SRC="bullet.gif" ALIGN=CENTER> Social Events<BR>
<IMG SRC="bullet.gif" ALIGN=CENTER> Flying Events/Competitions<BR>
```

New Icons

On the CD

Many sites also use icons to label new additions to their home page. This helps visitors quickly locate recent changes and information since their last visit. A whole stack of New icons can be found in the /GRAPHICS/ICONS/NEW subdirectory on the CD-ROM in the back of this book. See how the flying club home page uses the New icon (and bullets) in figure 6.15.

Fig. 6.15
Here's the spiffed up flying club page, bullets and all.

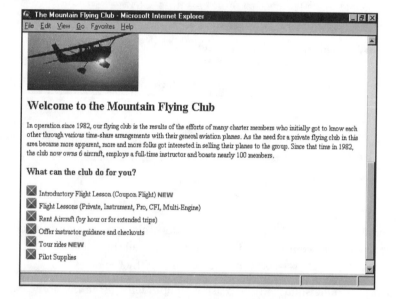

Tip

Make sure you don't leave a New icon on your page for months and months. It's common practice to label a new item on your home page for the first month or so it's on there. After that, ditch the New icon for that item.

Construction Icons

Construction icons became popular awhile ago, when everybody's home page was new and constantly being modified. These cute icons labeled the Web page as changing often, or not yet finished.

Nowadays, they're not quite as common, but you still see them on new pages regularly. You can also find construction icons in the /GRAPHICS/ICONS/ CONSTRUCT subdirectory on the included CD.

> **Note**
>
> This is a personal preference, but I recommend against construction icons when possible. After all, you should be constantly updating your pages, right? So there's no point in using construction icons to let people know that the page changes. They'll check once or twice to find out on their own. And if you're using the construction icon as a placeholder for an option you'll add later, consider just not introducing the option until you're ready. It's annoying to click a link, only to find out that the author hasn't finished that part of the Web site yet.

Navigation Icons

Navigation icons are probably the most useful icons to professional HTML developers, and least useful to people creating a basic home page. They come in handy when you have a large Web site with lots of pages linked together. Since your home page is likely to be simple, you may not find navigation icons to be very useful.

These types of icons usually come in the form of arrows pointing one way or another. These arrows allow you to symbolize which way to go to bring up the next Web page. For example, if you were reading a book on the WWW, you'd probably see three icons on each page—a left arrow, right arrow, and a home icon. The left arrow would bring you to the preceding page, the right arrow brings up the next page, while the home icon would take you to the very beginning of the book. This saves you the trouble of picking your way through the back and forward buttons on the AOL toolbar.

Navigation icons are really only useful if you are trying to tie together multiple pages at a site. See Chapter 8, "Cool Ways to Customize Your Web Page," for more ideas on using navigation icons on your pages. Also check out the /GRAPHICS/ICONS/NAVIGATE subdirectory on the CD for lots of unique navigational icons.

Give Your Web Page a Background

One of the neatest features of the recent HTML 3.2 standard (and Netscape-compatible browsers) is the ability to control what the background of your document looks like. Instead of creating pages that only have the standard gray color behind text, you can change the background by placing an image behind your text for adding a color, texture, and fun to your page.

Using Background Images

Patterned background graphics can give a cool effect to your home page when used properly. A typical background pattern is simply a GIF image that's tiled over and over again to cover the entire background (it's like wallpapering the page). Your text and images are placed on top of the background image.

On the CD

Background patterns are added with the BACKGROUND attribute to the <BODY> tag. Simply add BACKGROUND="YOUR.GIF" to your <BODY> tag, and HTML 3.x compatible browsers will load your image automatically. You'll find hundreds of sample background images on the CD. The following code uses the background BACK.JPG for the flight club home page (see fig. 6.16):

```
<BODY BACKGROUND="BACK.JPG">
```

Fig. 6.16
Background patterns add a lot of texture to Web pages.

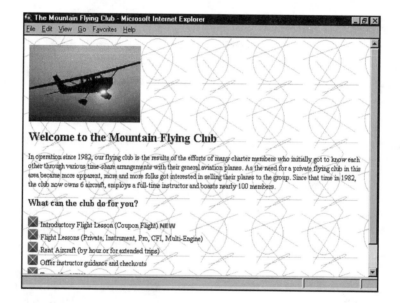

Background Problems

Before you go hog wild adding background patterns, it's important to keep some issues in mind. Generally speaking, you'll want to use very light background patterns, especially since many HTML 3.x compatible browsers don't always give you control over both the background and the text colors. Remember that nearly all graphical browsers default to black text. To reach the widest audience, I'd recommend only using backgrounds that look good with black text over top of them.

Also, adding background images to a home page can considerably increase the amount of time it takes for visitors to download your page to their PCs. All the background images on the included CD are reasonable to use, size-wise. If you use other background patterns, or make your own, make sure you limit them to a maximum of about 10 KB. ❖

CHAPTER 7

Linking Web Pages Together

A Web page without links to other WWW spots is an isolated island. Once people visit, there's no way for them to get to other places on the Web—or, for that matter, leave the page! Since you don't want to isolate people on your home page, it's a good idea to include links to several other pages that exist on the WWW. That way you can help build the spider-like Web yourself.

Linking Web pages together is the most basic feature of the WWW. Any document can contain a link to another WWW document using a special HTML tag. This chapter is all about using these hypertext link tags to connect Web pages to one another. You'll learn the proper way to link your home page to other HTML documents anywhere on the Internet.

Understanding Hypertext Links

As a Web surfer, you've probably already experienced hypertext links on the Web pages you've seen. While scanning through a page, you notice some text appears in blue and is underlined. Text displayed like this is called *hot text* because clicking it links you automatically to another Web page.

Every URL (Uniform Resource Locator) requires three parts: a protocol, an Internet site, and a file and path name. In this chapter, I talk about HTTP, the default WWW protocol (a *protocol* is the way two computers speak to each other). You must supply the Internet site and file and path name.

For example, my home page URL is **http://members.aol.com/tstauffer/**. Translated into English, this means you must use the special WWW communication method (**http**) to connect over the Internet to computers at America Online that serve up members' Web pages (**members.aol.com**). Then you find my home page in my own directory (**tstauffer**).

Hypertext links are often used because they can transparently join two documents on opposite sides of the world. Documents and files on the Internet are referred to by their own unique address: an URL. To link two documents to each other, home page designers add an URL on their Web pages. Using an URL is like addressing e-mail. The Internet computers understand how to translate the URL and find the exact spot to which it should connect.

If the home page is in New York, it doesn't matter if the linked document is in the Bronx, or New Zealand—the WWW treats it the same way. The browser uses each URL to find documents on the Internet and bring them up automatically for you. As a Web surfer, you don't have to worry about using URLs, connecting to Internet sites around the world, or locating the correct document, since browsers generally take care of all that hassle for you.

With the WWW, you can link to HTML documents (like your home page), files (via FTP), Internet Newsgroups (like UseNet), and even popular information sources such as Gopher and the Wide Area Information Server (WAIS) directly from your home page.

> **Note**
>
> This chapter teaches you how to link HTML documents to each other. See "Linking to Other Internet Resources" in Chapter 8 for instructions on creating hypertext links to the other popular Internet protocols from your home page.

On your home page, every link must be created one at a time. You get to decide what text to make hot and, more importantly, toward what URL you want the hot text to direct the browser. You can add as many (or as few) links to your home page as you like and organize them in any fashion.

Anatomy of a Link

Linking Web pages to each other isn't very difficult, but you've got to understand the HTML syntax and how to add links to your home page.

Just like every other HTML element, links have their own HTML tag. This tag (called the anchor tag, <A>) lets you specify which file you are linking to, what text should be hot or underlined when viewing your home page through a browser, and then wraps everthing up with an "off" tag (</A>).

Here's an example of what a link on my home page looks like in HTML:

```
<A HREF="http://www.mcp.com/que/">Que Publishing</A>
```

Figure 7.1 shows how the same link appears on my page.

Hot text

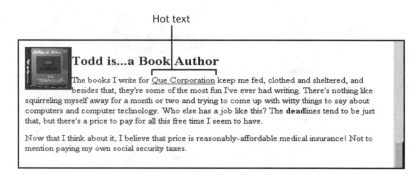

Fig. 7.1
Since Que Publishing is hot text, it appears underlined. Clicking the text with your mouse will cause Que's home page to load in the browser window.

Creating a Link

Now that you've read about using links and have seen them in action, let's add one to your home page. We will add two different (but similar) kinds of links to your page.

First, I'm going to show you how to link *local documents* to your page. A local document is one which is at the same Internet location as your home page. Local documents are easier to link to because you don't have to know the complete URL, only its filename and path relative to your home page.

Using almost the identical process, you'll also learn to link documents together when they are located at different spots on the WWW. For this type of link, you need to add the entire URL to your home page.

Linking to Local Web Pages

Often you will have multiple HTML documents in one spot. There may be too much information to put in one document, so you split it up into several different HTML files. On your main Web page, you want to link to each of those separate documents easily and quickly. Maybe your home page is set up like a table of contents, linking to several different pages.

The text *Our Planes* appears on my flight club's home page, and I'd like to make that a link to the pages I've created that show pictures and information about the different planes available for rent from the club. To add a link to the Plane page using HotDog, follow these steps:

1. Type the text you want highlighted as a link to your page. I'll type **Our Planes** on my flying club home page.

2. Select and highlight that text with your mouse and click the File Manager icon to bring up the HotDog File Manager dialog box (see fig. 7.2).

II

Creating a Basic Web Page

Fig. 7.2
The built-in file manager lets you link your home page to any document you select.

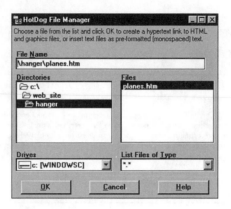

3. Using the mouse, I'll select the file I want to link to. I'm going to select PLANES.HTM from the HANGER subdirectory.

4. In the File Name text box at the top of the dialog box, delete the C: or whatever drive letter and colon appear, leaving just the directory and filename path. (You may also need to delete the first directory name— e.g., C:\WEB_SITE—if you won't be using that directory once you upload your files to AOL.)

5. Click OK to add the link. HotDog creates the HTML link automatically with the following code:

```
<A HREF="/hanger/planes.htm">Our Planes</A>
```

See figure 7.3 for how the new flying club home page looks once I've added this new link.

Fig. 7.3
Here's the flying club home page with the new link added.

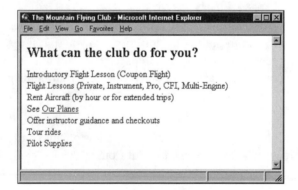

Caution

When you create a local link on your PC, remember to use the exact same filename and path structure you'll use when you upload your files to your AOL My Place directory. If, in my example, I forget to create a HANGER subdirectory on my Internet site, the user's browser won't be able to properly find the linked file.

Also, you have to account for the fact that HotDog assumes you're developing your pages directly on the Web server. For instance, when I browsed for the PLANES.HTM file, HotDog responded by filling in the File Name text box in the File Manager dialog box. It entered C:\WEB_SITE\HANGER\PLANES.HTM as its path statement.

But I need to change that so it will work correctly once I upload the file to my AOL Web site (the HANGER subdirectory will be located directly within the TSTAUFFER directory, where my home page will reside). So, I had to edit that path statement to \HANGER\PLANES.HTM.

Now, with this information, HotDog properly creates the link. Otherwise HotDog would create a link like FILE:///C¦/WEB_SITE/HANGER/INDEX.HTM which will not work correctly from the My Place directory (or, as a matter of fact, from most any Web server).

Linking Elsewhere on the WWW

The other trick is to link your home page to other HTML documents that reside on WWW sites other than your own. Linking to these sites requires you to know the full URL to the document, not just the filename and path as in the previous section.

The link, however, looks the same. You still use the <A HREF=> and </A> tags to surround hot text. When you are linking to other HTML documents on the Web, your URL will always start with **http://**.

That's so the user's browser knows that it needs to communicate with the distant server using the Hypertext (Web) protocol. The rest of the URL consists of the Internet path of the site, and then the full name of the document to which you are linking.

Tip

By default, if you don't specify a filename, most Web servers automatically load the file INDEX.HTML (or INDEX.HTM) when linking to a site. Since it is a WWW standard, nearly every site has an INDEX.HTML file. At my site, my home page is named INDEX.HTML.

As an example, I'm going to add a link to the Yahoo list of other flying clubs that have Web sites to the Mountain Flying Club Page.

Choose Insert, Simple URL from the HotDog menu bar to bring up the Insert URL dialog box shown in figure 7.4.

Fig. 7.4
HotDog lets you insert a URL in the same fashion as you added a graphic in the last chapter.

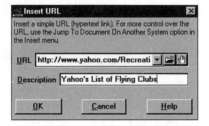

Type the full URL of the HTML document you are linking to in the URL box. The URL of the Yahoo Flying Club list is **http://www.yahoo.com/ Recreation/Aviation/Clubs/**.

Then type **Yahoo's List of Flying Clubs** as the text that will appear hot in the user's browser in the Description box.

When you are finished, click OK to add the link to your document. The following line of HTML was added to the flying home page:

```
<A HREF="http://www.yahoo.com/Recreation/Aviation/Clubs/
">Yahoo's List of Flying Clubs</A>
```

With the link added, you can easily jump from one page to another as shown in figures 7.5 and 7.6.

Fig. 7.5
Clicking the link in the Mountain Flying Club home page brings up the linked document.

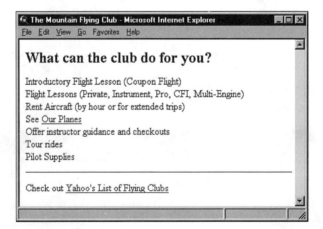

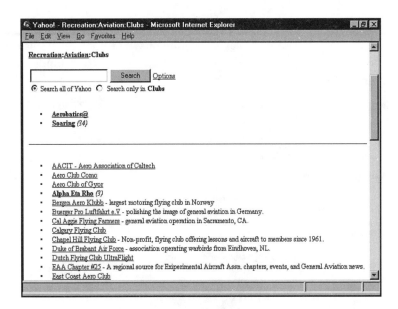

Fig. 7.6
This is the linked
document from
Yahoo's Web site.

Using Images as Links

Not only can you use text to link to other WWW pages, but you can use images as well. In the last chapter, I explained how to add images to your home page. Now you'll learn how to make them "clickable." That's when you click your mouse on an image and a linked WWW document appears.

You can link an image on your home page to another HTML document in the exact same fashion as you linked text. The only difference is that instead of designating text to be hot, you are assigning an image. In most browsers, a blue box appears around the image and links visitors to a different page when they click their mouse anywhere on the picture. You can use any kind of image, picture, or icon (except for background images) to link WWW documents together.

Tip

Using images to link pages together is very common. But make sure you use recognizable images so that visitors have some idea where the link will go. For example, if you are going to link your home page to a list of your favorite songs, use an icon that is music-related. It's also extremely important to use the ALT keyword when linking images. This ensures that visitors that can't see images will still be able to use your links.

I link several graphics in my home page to different Web sites. For example, I have a photo of a Que book displayed prominently. The book cover image is linked to the publisher's home page so that if you click it, you'll immediately be brought to the Que site on the WWW.

This link is the exact same as the one I used at the very beginning of the chapter—with one change. Instead of typing "Que Publishing" between the <A HREF=> and </A> tags, I placed the HTML code for displaying an image there instead. Below is the HTML code, and figure 7.7 shows how the newly linked image appears:

```
<A HREF="http://www.mcp.com/que/">
<IMG SRC="inetmac.gif" ALIGN=LEFT>
</A>
```

Fig. 7.7
Now this image is wired to Que's Web site.

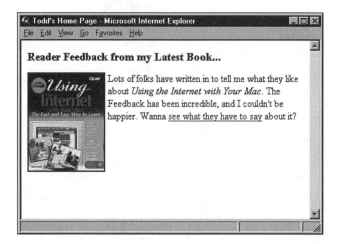

To accomplish this in HotDog, start by inserting the image, as discussed in Chapter 6. Then, highlight the HTML code for the image and select Insert, Simple URL from the HotDog menu. Now, just enter the URL for this link in the Insert URL dialog box.

> **Note**
>
> With some more advanced HTML programming, you can also create clickable images that take you to different pages depending on where in the image you selected. These types of graphics are called *image maps* and are significantly more complicated to create and maintain. For more information about using image maps, see "What Is an Image Map?" in Chapter 9.

Using Targets on Your Home Page

Now that you're an accomplished HTML linker, you can connect your home page to any other file on the Internet. However, there are a few other uses for the <A> and </A> anchor tags—for instance, as internal document references and pointers, or *target* links.

Here's what I mean. Let's say you picked up a large book because you wanted to read the contents of Chapter 26. You don't want to have to flip through and scan the first 25 chapters just to locate Chapter 26 in your book. Instead, you'd go to the table of contents, find out what page Chapter 26 begins on, and go straight there.

Target links work in a similar way. When you have a large HTML document, you can add anchors to various points in the document. In this example, if the large book was one really big HTML file, you'd probably have a target at the beginning of each chapter. At the very beginning of the HTML file, you'd have a table of contents that would link to each separate target in your file (one for each chapter). When you click a link labeled Chapter 26, the browser would take you automatically to where the Chapter 26 target is in the same file. You wouldn't have to scroll through countless pages of information.

Pretty nifty, huh? Targets work the same way as do links to other documents on the WWW, except that you are linking to internal spots of a single document instead. Just like regular links, you can have as many targets and tags as you want.

> **Note**
>
> Instead of using the name anchors, many people also split their Web page into many separate pages. See "Expanding Your Home Page into a Home Site" in Chapter 8 for more information on how to do this.

Creating and Naming a Target

On your home page, you can add named anchor tags wherever you like. Each tag you add allows you to jump directly to that spot with a link. For this example, I have four different target tags and links on the Flying Club's Services page.

In HTML, targets use the following format:

```
<A NAME="Target_Name"> Document Text </A>
```

Notice that we're using a new attribute for <A> in this example: NAME. The NAME attribute tells the browser that this is a target, not an actual link. Since it's an internal reference, it won't change the appearance of text it surrounds.

HotDog lets you add targets to your page easily. Highlight the text you want to mark as a target, and click the Target icon to bring up the Enter Target ID dialog box (see fig. 7.8). I'm going to highlight one of the Services page's four headings talking about the flight club's services, shown in the following HTML code:

```
<H3>Flight Instruction</H3>
```

> **Tip**
>
> You don't have to place your target around text if you don't want to. In that case, don't highlight any text; just move your cursor to the spot you'd like the target to be added and then click the Target icon.

Fig. 7.8
Place your target/
anchor label here.

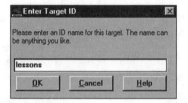

Type the name of your target and click OK. I'll type **lessons** for my example. The following lines of HTML appear:

```
<A NAME="lessons"><H3>Flight Instruction</H3></A>
```

There's now a target on the Services page at the beginning of the section that discusses flight lessons.

> **Tip**
>
> Make sure that you put the target tag at the very top of where you want to jump, because browsers place the line with the target at the very top of their screen. If your target is below your headline, your users wouldn't see it when they jump to that spot (they could scroll up and see it though).

Linking to the Target

Once you have created all of the targets you need for your page, it's time to create your own table of contents, or links to each specific target.

Go to the top of your home page in HotDog and click the Internal icon at the top of the screen to bring up the Select Hypertext Target dialog box, shown in figure 7.9.

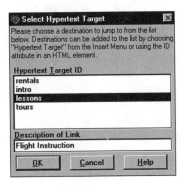

Fig. 7.9
All of the targets in this HTML document are listed here.

Choose the target you want to link to in the Hypertext Target ID box and type the text that will link you to that target in the Description of Link box. When you are finished, click OK and HotDog will add your HTML link for you, like the following:

```
<A HREF="#lessons">Learn to Fly</A>
```

Notice the # in the HREF keyword? That symbol tells the user's browser to look for a target instead of a separate HTML document. Most browsers display the hot text just like any other link (see fig. 7.10). But instead of looking for a different file or going to a separate WWW site, the browser looks only in the HTML file it is displaying for the named target.

Note

You can link directly to targets in any HTML document on the WWW. For instance, if you wanted to link directly to the information on my personal Web site that discusses my freelance rates, you'd add the following piece of HTML to your home page:

```
<A HREF="http://members.aol.com/tstauffer/contract.html#Rates">
Link to Todd's Freelance Info</A>
```

To link to a specific target on another page, view the HTML source code of that document (in Internet Explorer, choose View, Source from the menu) and find the target you want to link to.

Fig. 7.10
The flying club
service page now
has targets and
links added to it.

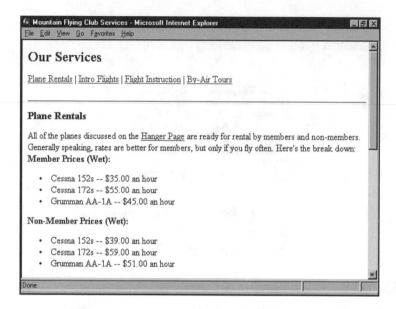

Caution

Linking to targets on other pages is sometimes not a good idea. They tend to change
often, since Web authors often decide to reorganize into a Web site once they feel
they have too many target links on the same document.

Organize Your Links with Lists

It's important to keep your links organized so that they're understandable
and easy to use. You'll find that, as you add more and more links to your
page, it's easy to let them get unorganized and fall into disarray. Every time
you add new HTML to your home page, you need to make sure that the page
is still easy to read and organized.

One popular method for keeping your links organized is using an HTML list.
As you saw in Chapter 5, lists help present many different pieces of information in a crisp, bulleted (or numbered) format. Lists work perfectly when you
want to include a bunch of links on your home page.

To create an unordered list of links, all you have to do is use the standard
<LI> tag, along with the <UL> (or <OL>) tag. Let each link use a separate <LI>
tag so that you have only one link per line. I guarantee that a simple list will

do more for organizing a bunch of links than practically any other way you could organize your page (see fig. 7.11).

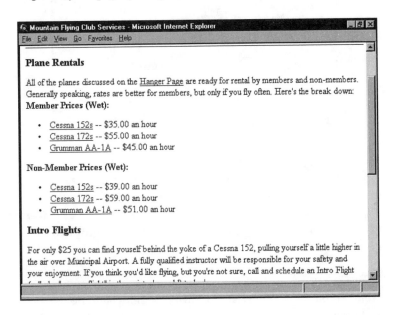

Fig. 7.11
Using a numbered or bulleted list for HTML links makes things look cleaner on your page.

Useful Linking Tips

Knowing how to add WWW links to your home page adds a powerful dimension to your HTML authoring repertoire. Along with this increased power and flexibility comes the opportunity to make your home page much more confusing and difficult to use for people who stop by for a visit.

Don't Over Link

Nothing is more confusing than stopping by a Web page with 200 words of text and 180 of them are linked to different spots on the WWW (see fig. 7.12). Since linked text appears underlined and in blue, having too many links in a paragraph (or on a page) makes it completely unreadable. No one will want to stop by.

Link Specific/Descriptive Words

Although the WWW relies on links that connect pieces of information with each other, try to make your links transparent. Here's an example of what I mean. The following paragraph does not have a transparent link (I marked the links in bold):

Fig. 7.12
I get a headache
just looking at
this page!

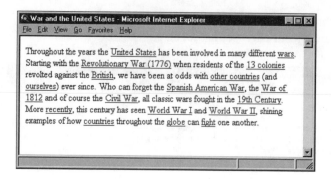

We offer many useful services for the professional and novice aviator at Mountain Flying Club, along with the type of atmosphere you'd expect from a group of folks dedicated to the love of flying. If you're just getting started, our full-time professional instructor here at the **Mountain Flying Club** offers an introductory flight lesson at only $35 for an hour of flight.

Try this text instead:

We offer many useful services for the professional and novice aviator at Mountain Flying Club, along with the type of atmosphere you'd expect from a group of folks dedicated to the love of flying. If you're just getting started, our full-time professional instructor here at the Mountain Flying Club offers an **introductory flight lesson** at only $35 for an hour of flight.

The highlighted text that marks a link for your users needs to be descriptive enough that they know where they're going. In the first example, using Mountain Flying Club as the linked text is confusing, since the reader is already on a page about the Mountain Flying Club. The link is actually about the flight lesson, so that's the text that should be linked.

Caution

One of my major criticisms of Web page creators is that they often highlight useless pieces of text as the link to another Web site. Of course, the most notorious culprits are the words *click* and/or *here*. Try to avoid using those words as links.

Even if you don't use "click here" as hot text on your page, you still need to be careful when choosing text to link to other pages. Here's a trick for doing it. Imagine that the text you choose as hot text has to stand on its own (with no other text surrounding it). Would it still make sense? In my example, **introductory flight lesson** would make sense all by itself or in a bulleted list.

Describe Large Links

Whenever you link your home page to larger graphics, files, audio bites, or video clips (even extremely large text files), you should let visitors know about the potential file size before they click the link. Large files take a while to download. For instance, it's very appropriate to create hot text like:

```
<A HREF="skiing.mov">QuickTime of Steve Skiing (250 KB)</A>
```

I'll talk more about this in Chapter 8.

Keep Your Links Current

As you get more experienced and continue to build your home page, you're likely to compile an entire collection of links to various parts of the Web. Occasionally, these links become obsolete. The distant Web page may be deleted or move to another site. Whatever the reason, you've got a decent chance that some of your links will become obsolete every few months.

Visitors who stop by and see an interesting link will be using the link provided on your home page, only to find that the Web page you've linked to no longer exists. If you are going to have many links on your home page, you should periodically check them all to make sure they are pointing to current documents. If not, change them to reflect the new site or delete them from your page. ❖

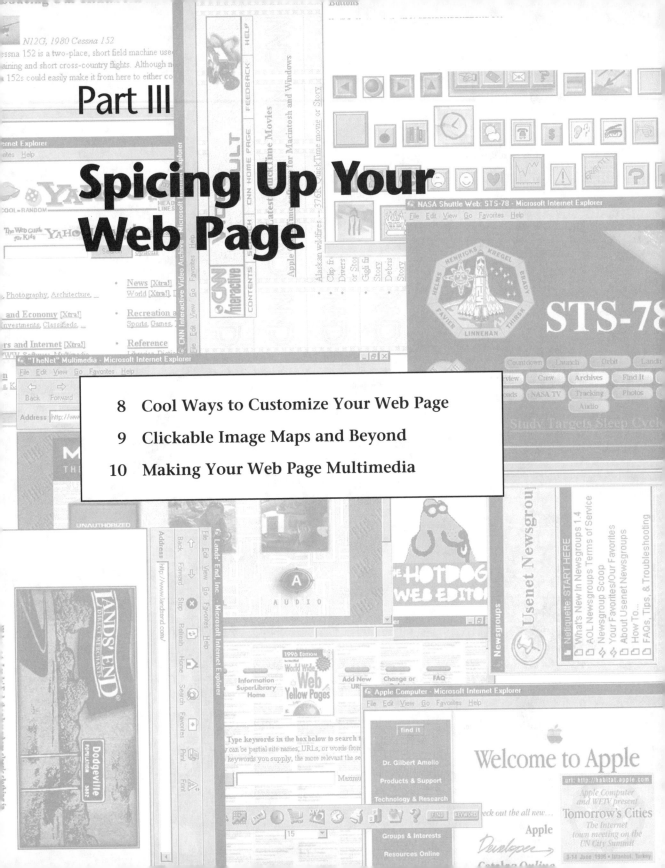

Part III

Spicing Up Your Web Page

CHAPTER 8

Cool Ways to Customize Your Web Page

Remember when you bought your last car? You went to the dealer's lot, haggled over a few bucks, and drove off the lot. You had a nice car, but I'm sure you wanted to add a few personal (and cool) customizations to it. Some people add CD players or alarms, while others add a sunroof or neon lights to their car—and don't forget the fuzzy dice! These personalized customizations are why every car is different and unique.

Right now, you've got a home page just driven straight off the lot. In this chapter, I'll show you how you can customize it to fit your own particular needs and wants. You can modify your standard home page into your own customized vehicle.

This chapter introduces you to a potpourri of great things you can do with your home page. I cover a diverse set of topics, none too complicated to start using immediately.

Expanding Your Home Page into a Home Site

When you left home as a teenager or young adult, you probably moved into a small, single-room apartment—one where you could afford to pay the rent and utilities. You didn't have much furniture or decorations to arrange on the walls, but sooner or later, you realized that you needed to move to a larger apartment and, eventually, perhaps, to a house.

Just as your first apartment always got messy and cluttered, eventually you will have too much information to fit on a single home page. While a basic home page might serve most of your needs, once you start adding all of your personal and professional interests, toss in several images and multimedia clips, and create links to Web pages all over the Internet, you may notice that your home page has become large and unwieldy. That's when it's time to expand your horizons and change your home page into a home site.

You'll still have a home page—that's the main starting point for visitors looking for information about you—but now your home page is linked to several other HTML documents pertaining to you. Combined together, I call this set of HTML documents your *home site*.

Why Split Up Your Home Page?

There are two important reasons for splitting your home page into a home site. The first is that it makes it easier for visitors to get the information that they want. If a potential employer stops by your home page, he or she doesn't really want to spend several minutes downloading text and images of your family; they want to see your resumé and work experience. If all of these aspects are separate documents, users can choose to see only the information they really want. This adds more control for your visitors.

The second, and more selfish reason (it was my reason for splitting), is so you can add more spiffy graphics and personal information. My home page was already overburdened with graphics and multimedia files. Adding more would have made it practically unreadable for most WWW visitors. When I split my page up into many pages, I was able to double the amount of graphics I could use. Practically every page of mine has a graphic or multimedia file of some sort.

Design Your Home Site Correctly

Before you split up your home page, you've got to come up with a plan. Remember way back in Chapter 2, where I talked about designing your single page appearance? This is the same process, except you're deciding the structure of your site and how your pages will link together.

Below, I've sketched out four possible ways you can choose to link your documents together. Each of these methods has its advantages and disadvantages in certain situations. You can choose whichever one of the following works best for your home page:

- **Standard**—In this format, your home page links to each of the other documents in your home site, and documents all link directly back to your home page. This is the easiest and most common way to create a Web site.

- **Waterfall**—Your documents are linked in a predefined order so that there is only one path through all of your pages. Water can only flow in one direction, and so can your visitors.

■ **Skyscraper**—To get to room 2676 in the Empire State Building, you've got to board the elevator and choose the 26th floor before you can walk down the hall to your location. In the Skyscraper model, some of your pages can only be read if visitors follow the right path.

■ **Web**—All of the pages in your site are linked to one another, allowing you to visit virtually any single page from another. This method is confusing when it gets out of hand, but is popular when your document links are used with moderation.

> **Tip**
>
> Incidentally, with my home site, I use a hybrid of these methods. The overall organization of my site follows the Web style, but I've found that as the site grows, I'm occassionally adding pages following the Skyscraper style—that is, some of my pages are only accessible from some others. Once a site reaches a certain size, it becomes impossible for all but the most primary pages to be linked together in a Web.

Splitting Your Page

Once you've decided on a home site structure, it's time to actually split your pages. Using HotDog, you can choose File, Save As from the menu and create new HTML files.

Try to give your files descriptive names so it's easier to make changes in the future. Having files named page1.htm, page2.htm, page3.htm, and so on aren't nearly as useful as resume.htm, personal.htm, and work.htm.

> **Note**
>
> The AOL My Place file system supports extended file names, so you can name your files something like online_resume.html or cool_links.htm if you feel like it. Remember that the names you use when you create the pages (and the names you use for links) have to be exactly the same as the names you use once you upload to My Place.

Make sure you add the <HTML>, <HEAD>, and <BODY> tags to each new page, as well as a new <TITLE> for the document. You have to go through the same motions as you did when you originally created your home page.

Each Web page that you create should not assume that the visitor came directly from your home page. Your separate Web pages can be linked from other sites. Each Web page should be self-contained and not missing important information (like your name) that people who linked to it might want to know.

Also, each of your Web pages should have a standard footer at the bottom that tells visitors who created the Web page, when it was last updated, and who to contact for more information. In fact, you might remember that I told you one of the most important sections to include on your home page is the <ADDRESS> section—that holds true here as well. In addition, it is also a good idea to include a link back to your home page to make navigating your site easier. Here's my footer in HTML:

```
<A HREF="http://members.aol.com/tstauffer/">Back to Todd's
Home Page</A><P>
<ADDRESS>
Last Updated Aug. 13, 1996 by
<A HREF="mailto:tstauffer@aol.com">Todd Stauffer</A><BR>
tstauffer@aol.com
</ADDRESS>
```

Figure 8.1 shows how the footer looks on one of my pages.

Fig. 8.1
This is a standard footer that does the trick nicely.

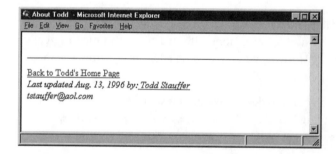

Tip

Don't forget to remove your HTML targets. (We discussed targets in the section titled "Using Targets on Your Home Page" in Chapter 7.) When you're splitting your pages into smaller, easier chunks to read, targets are usually no longer necessary because each section is now a separate file—or, they at least need to be edited to reflect the new URLs.

Linking Your Pages Together

With your pages split, it's time to link your home page to each one of them. Make sure you link your pages together in an order that would make sense to anyone who would visit your home page.

For example, I have an online resumé page and one detailing my freelance rates and specialties. I could have linked my freelance information Web page to my resumé (under Work Experience) instead of linking the freelance info directly to my home page. Even though this makes sense logically, most visitors would never even know I had the freelance info available unless they looked at my resumé first. I chose to make it a link directly on my home page.

You have several options for linking your home site together. I use a small listing of control links at the top of every page that allows the user to get to nearly any other. It's nice because it's text-based, doesn't take up much real estate on the page, and is consistant from page to page:

```
<h5>
<a href="index.html">Index</a> ¦
<a href="about.html">About Todd </a> ¦
<a href="contract.html">Freelance Info</a> ¦
<a href="radio.html">Radio Show</a> ¦
<a href="resume.html">Resume</a> ¦
<a href="feedback.html">Reader Feedback</a>
</h5>
```

> **Note**
>
> Notice how most of my HTML documents are located in the same directory as my original file. You can organize your HTML files into whichever directory structure you choose, but using one directory when uploading to My Place is probably easiest, unless your site is very large.

See figure 8.2 to see how this small control strip of links looks on my pages.

Fig. 8.2
The links look the same as they did when all of my information was in the same file.

Tracking How Many People Visit Your Home Page

One of the most popular requests for new home page owners is the ability to figure out how many people stop by their page. Without this information, you won't know if your home page is as popular as a Manhattan night club, or as barren as the Sahara desert.

In most cases, you've got to track your visitors yourself. There are several different ways to add an incremental counter to your home page. These counters keep track of every time someone visits your page and add that increasing number to your home page.

Adding the AOL Counter

Although AOL doesn't permit much of the more advanced programming and data management that is possible on some Web sites, it does have a few extras for your personal home site. For instance, a simple odometer-style "hit" counter, for including on your home page, is available for you to use.

The hit counter keeps track of how many folks stop by your site by simply adding to the number in a simple document that's saved in your My Place directory. The counter itself is a graphic, but the graphic varies, since it needs to look like a car's odometer counting up the number of hits.

Adding the counter is simple. You'll probably want to put the counter some-where closer to the bottom of your home page, but that's up to you. I'd also recommend just using the counter on your home page—the page that intro-duces your site. Putting the counter on other pages is generally redundant, and it wastes your users' time when the graphic has to be downloaded every time they move to another page.

Here's how you add the AOL counter:

```
<img src="/cgi-bin/counter?screenname">
```

For *screenname*, substitute the screen name that you use for the Web site—it should be identical to the directory name you use in your My Place URL. For instance, my counter works like this:

```
<img src="/cgi-bin/counter?tstauffer">
```

I like to explain the counter to my users, but it really doesn't matter that much—Web browsers are probably getting used to counters by now. Here's all the code I use for my counter:

```
This site visited: <img src="/cgi-bin/counter?tstauffer"> times
since Feb. 29, 1996.
```

Figure 8.3 shows you what that looks like on my home page.

This site visited: 00000127 times since Feb. 29, 1996.

Copyright Todd A. Stauffer 1996. All Rights Reserved. Do not duplicate without permission.

These pages are HTML 2.0 friendly!

Fig. 8.3
Here's AOL's car odometer-style hit counter for members' pages.

Adding a Web-based Counter

While browsing the Web one day, I found a simple site that lets anyone who has a home page add an incremental counter to his or her page(s) by just adding a simple HTML link (like the kind you created in Chapter 7). Nothing fancy—this counter requires no time-consuming support or special knowledge of advanced HTML code.

Once you insert a link to the counter on your home page, the counter increments by one every time a visitor stops by. You link your home page to a database that counts your home page visitors.

Anyone can have their own personal counter added to their Web page. For more information, visit **http://www.digits.com** and you'll learn step-by-step how to add a link to your Web page with a single HTML tag.

> **Tip**
>
> You should place this link towards the bottom of your document. Browsers tend to load pages from the top down, and it takes several additional seconds to link to the counter page and return with the current visitor number. Placing it on the bottom of your page makes it easier for visitors to ignore that short wait, because they can see the rest of your page.

Linking to Other Internet Resources

When I was writing this book, I needed to stay in constant communication with Que, my publisher. I was on the phone with them often and regularly exchanged e-mail messages as well. When simple words weren't enough, I would fax information to them immediately, while other times, Federal Express became an important crutch. All these types of communication were part of a normal day.

The Internet works in a similar way, only on a much bigger scale. Thousands of computers need to constantly talk to each other and exchange information. Using various communication standards, or Internet protocols, computers communicate with each other in several different ways. Each of these different protocols has its own special uses, features, and advantages. I wouldn't use a fax machine to transmit a 100-page manuscript, and likewise, I wouldn't try to e-mail a huge file to my publisher—there are better, more efficient methods of sending that information.

In Chapter 7, I introduced links and showed you how to connect two HTML documents together using the HTTP protocol. The HTTP protocol was developed specifically for the World Wide Web, and is the most common protocol used to communicate between Internet servers and Web browser applications like Internet Explorer.

But they're not the only protocols that browsers support. And, by extension, links to nearly every Internet protocol can be added to your Web page. They work the same way as the links I talked about in Chapter 7, only you need to know the correct URL to use the various Internet protocols.

Using HotDog to Add Internet URLs

It's easy to link your home page to other Internet services with HotDog. Click the Internet icon in the HotDog menu bar to bring up the Create HyperText Link dialog box (see fig. 8.4).

Fig. 8.4
HotDog lists all the possible link types you can create.

Choose the type of link you want to create and HotDog will prompt you for the full address of the site you want to link. Figure 8.5 shows the Choose Newsgroup dialog box that appears when you click Go to a UseNet Newsgroup.

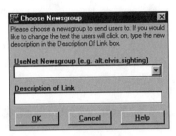

Fig. 8.5
HotDog adds a graphical interface to building your links.

I recommend using HotDog to build your Internet links. All you have to type is the link address and the text description you want to make "hot," and HotDog builds the link for you. The following sections describe how to add several of the most popular types of Internet links to your pages.

FTP

There are millions of different files available on the Internet. Everything from the latest shareware games to catalogs of recipes can be downloaded directly to your home computer using *FTP (File Transfer Protocol)*.

Files that are accessible via FTP can be added directly to your home page. This convenience allows visitors the ability to download files without loading a separate FTP program. To add an FTP link, choose Go to an FTP Server from the Create HyperText Link dialog box.

The FTP URL of HotDog, the Web editor used in this book, is **ftp:// ftp.sausage.com/pub/hd253.exe**.

> **Caution**
>
> This FTP URL is meant only as an example; if and when HotDog is updated, this URL will probably change as well. Of course, that's a risk you run anytime you add an URL to your Web page.

Here's how I added that address to my home page:

```
<A HREF="ftp://ftp.sausage.com/pub/hd253.exe"> Download the HotDog
Web Editor </A>
```

See, it's just like linking using the HTTP protocol, only with a different URL. In the browser, `Download the HotDog Web Editor` appears like any other link on your home page. When visitors click that link, their browsers automatically open up an FTP connection and download the specified file. See figure 8.6 for the window that appears in Internet Explorer when I click the FTP link.

Fig. 8.6
Internet Explorer notices this is an FTP protocol transmission, and asks me where I want the file saved.

> **Note**
>
> The method I've described here works only for anonymous FTP access. Anonymous FTP access allows anyone on the Internet to connect to a certain site and download files. Most FTP sites allow anonymous access.
>
> However, there may be times where you want to connect to a password-protected FTP site. If you needed to access a special FTP site that requires a password for access, your FTP URL would look like **ftp://userid:password@secret.agency.gov/pub/plans.exe**.
>
> You must specify the user ID and password when using a passworded FTP site.
>
> Be careful when adding password-protected FTP sites to your home page. Anyone who clicks the link will be able to visit that FTP site using your user ID and password. Links to non-anonymous FTP sites are best used for Web pages no one else will ever see.

News

On the Internet, thousands of UseNet newsgroups are available for text-based discussions, covering every topic imaginable. Whether you want to talk about popular music, gardening, or Windows 95, there's bound to be a newsgroup for you.

You can link your home page to as many different newsgroups as you'd like just by knowing the full newsgroup name. To add a newsgroup link to your Web page, choose Go to a UseNet Newsgroup from the Create HyperText Link dialog box. The URL to the newsgroup where new Web pages and tools are announced is **news:comp.infosystems.www.announce**.

To add this as a link to your home page, type the following HTML:

```
<LI><A HREF="news:comp.infosystems.www.announce">The USENET Web
Announcements Group</A>
```

After clicking the newsgroup link, the browser brings up a list of available articles that you can choose from. (Currently the AOL browser sends this UseNet request to the AOL newsreader, as in figure 8.7.) Click a message subject to read that particular newsgroup message.

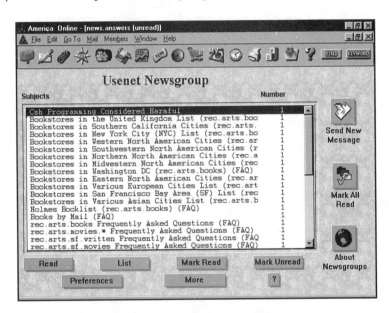

Fig. 8.7
This high-volume newsgroup always has new messages to read.

Gopher

Another popular Internet application is Gopher. Developed at the University of Minnesota (hence the name), Gopher is a text-based menu system that allows Internet sites to sort and organize vast quantities of information. You must step through various levels of menus to find the information you want at a Gopher site.

III

Spicing Up Your Web Page

Many Internet sites have Gopher menu systems, but they are increasingly less popular as more information migrates over to the Web. Gopher is text-only and not nearly as exciting to look at as a colorful Web page. Regardless, there is still a lot of information and activity using Gopher, and you may want to link some of that information to your Web pages. To include a Gopher link to your page, choose Go to a Gopher from the Create HyperText Link dialog box.

A sample Gopher URL that links you to the U.S. State Department Travel Advisory on France is **gopher://gopher.stolaf.edu:70/00/ Internet%20Resources/US State-Department-Travel-Advisories/ Current-Advisories/france**.

The following is the HTML code used when I added that link to my home page (see fig. 8.8):

```
<A HREF="gopher://gopher.stolaf.edu:70/00/Internet%20Resources/US-
State-Department-Travel-Advisories/Current-Advisories/
france">Gopher report on the US Travel Advisory on France</A>
```

Fig. 8.8
Gopher may not be as pretty as the Web, but still has a lot of current information.

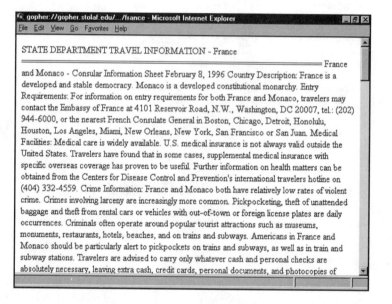

Note

Did you notice the **%20** in the previous Gopher URL? Web browsers don't know how to interpret spaces in their HTML links. You can get around that by replacing spaces with the text: **%20**. Web browsers know how to read and translate that special code automatically.

If by chance you need to add an actual percent (%) into your URL, replace it with the **%25** code.

E-mail

E-mail, or electronic mail, is the most popular way to communicate privately between users on the Internet. Usually, users must load a separate program to send e-mail across the Internet. But most Web browsers can manage to send you an e-mail message when you embed a special link in your pages. If a user clicks a mailto link, his or her browser will pop up a window designed to let the user compose an e-mail message and send it.

Most Web authors add an e-mail link to themselves at the bottom of their page so that visitors can easily send them questions or comments without switching back to their separate e-mail program. To include an e-mail link to your home page, choose Let the User Send Mail to Someone from the Create HyperText Link dialog box.

On my home page, I have an e-mail link to myself on many of my pages. My URL is **Mailto:tstauffer@aol.com**.

This URL tells the user's browser to bring up a blank e-mail message and address it to **tstauffer@aol.com**. (AOL's browser will bring up the AOL Compose Mail screen, as shown in figure 8.9). My HTML code appears as follows:

```
<A HREF="mailto:tstauffer@aol.com">Send e-mail to Todd</A>
```

Tip

I don't recommend replacing the <ADDRESS> section of your page with a mailto link. In fact, you should probably just add the mailto link to your current <ADDRESS> info. Since not all Web browsers will work correctly with the mailto command, you'll want your actual e-mail address available for them to cut-and-paste into their e-mail program.

Fig. 8.9
Now users can
quickly get a
message to you.

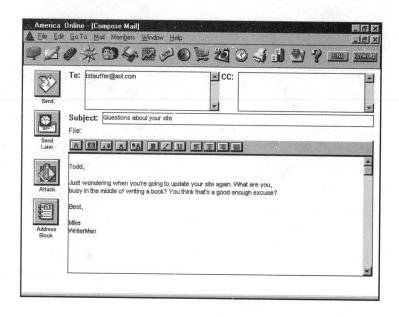

CHAPTER 9

Clickable Image Maps and Beyond

One of the coolest things we can add to our AOL-based home page is a clickable image map—but we have to do it in a special way. Generally speaking, there are two different types of clickable image maps: server-side and client-side. So what's the difference? And, while we're at it, what's an image map? Good questions. We'll talk about that in this chapter, then we'll see how to add an image map to our pages.

What is an Image Map?

Image maps are related to standard clickable images, with one major difference. When you link a regular image to another HTML file, it doesn't matter where the image is clicked—the same document always appears. Image maps are different. With an image map, you can link various parts of the image to different HTML files.

There are several good uses for image maps. For example, Italy might place a virtual map online. Using your mouse, you'd click whichever region or city of Italy you wanted to learn more about. Clicking Rome might bring up the Coliseum, and Pisa could link to that famous leaning tower. Or Boeing might place a picture of its new 777 plane on the Web. Visitors could click different parts of the cockpit to learn how the plane operates.

Take a look at figure 9.1 for a better understanding of what I mean. In this figure, I have three different shapes combined together. A standard image would link to the same file, no matter where on the image you clicked. With an image map defined, I can tell browsers to bring up a different file depending on which shape is clicked.

Fig. 9.1
These images—the triangle, rectangle, and circle—are clickable.

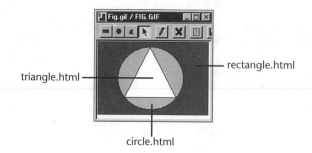

triangle.html

rectangle.html

circle.html

Virtually any image can become an image map—and they're not tough to create. With the right tools (and they're provided for you on the included CD), anyone can add an image map to their home page in a matter of minutes.

Image Maps Aren't New

If you've spent much time on the Web at all, you've probably encountered image maps. In fact, they're the basic method that most Web designers use to create graphical *interfaces* to their Web site. Using clickable maps allows a graphic designer to give a distinct feel to a Web site, making the visitor's stay a more exciting, more appealing one.

Apple Computer, for instance, uses a very conservative image map on its home page, and yet, as basic as it is, it gives a professional look to the site (see fig. 9.2). You can see this site at **http://www.apple.com/** to get a feel for image maps on your own. (Realize, though, that Apple tends to redesign its site every few months.)

Fig. 9.2
Apple Computer's Web site uses a very clean-looking image map (in the top left corner) to give users access to the entire site.

A little closer to home, the Que home page has a different feel to its image map, but it doesn't look any less professional. I like to think of this as an example of the higher-end of what can be accomplished with image maps (see fig. 9.3).

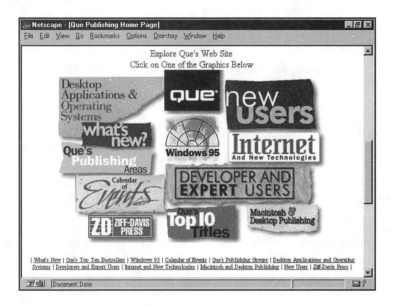

Fig. 9.3
Que Corporation (**http://www.mcp.com/que/**) isn't exactly a study in restraint, but it's a great example of an image map.

Client-Side versus Server-Side

What is new about image maps is the *client-side* image map specification. Up until recently, most image maps were *server-side* which, as you might guess, required input from the Web server computer. With client-side image maps, it's up to the browser to interpret the user's clicks. And that's good news for us, since we don't have access to our Web server—it's controlled by AOL.

A server-side image map actually requires two things: a *map server program* (running on the Web server computer) and a special *map definition* file (see fig. 9.4). In a nutshell, the browser interprets where the user clicked a server-side image map and sends it to the map server program. The map server program receives the coordinates for the point, looks them up in the map definition file, and returns the corresponding Web page to the browser.

Fig. 9.4

A typical map definition file. Notice the coordinates and the corresponding Web page names.

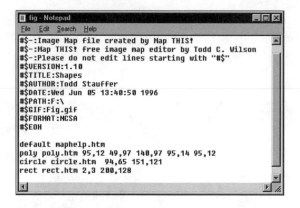

But, since AOL doesn't provide map server capabilties, you and I have to look somewhere else. That somewhere is Spyglass, Inc, the for-profit company that licenses new versions of Mosaic. Spyglass developed a client-side image map specification earlier this year, now incorporated into the HTML 3.2 standard.

Now, it's all the browser. In your HTML document, you can flag a particular image as an image map. Then, you enter the map definition information in that same HTML document. When a Spyglass-compatible (or HTML 3.2-compatible) browser notices the user clicking the client-side map, it looks up the coordinates itself, and then asks the Web server to send the appropriate page, just as it would for a normal link.

Who Supports Client-Side Maps?

To my knowledge, the only major browsers that currently support client-side image maps are Internet Explorer, Netscape, and versions of Spyglass Mosaic. While it's unfortunate that more browsers don't yet support client-side maps, it's also true that those three browsers make up over 85 percent of the browser market. I think you're pretty safe using client-side maps, especially since we'll also be adding some safeguards for folks who use non-compatible or text-based browsers.

Realize, though, that we're going beyond the HTML 2.0 specification with client-side image maps. (Server-side maps are supported by HTML 2.0.) If it's important to you to stay with the older, more widely-supported standard, then think twice about this chapter.

Creating Clickable Image Maps

We'll have to learn a little HTML for our new client-side image map. Creating client-side image maps isn't tough, but it does takes a little extra typing.

We've also got a neat trick up our sleeve—we get to borrow some tools from the server-side folks.

There are four basic steps in creating an image map. They are as follows:

1. Find a good image to use.

2. Using special image map software, you define which parts of the image will link to HTML documents.

3. You place the image in your HTML document and mark it as a client-side map.

4. Finally, you add the image map definition information to the HTML document.

Getting the Right Image

The first (and most difficult) step in creating an image map is finding the right image to use. Practically any type of picture, icon, or graphic can be an effective image map, but some make better choices than others. As a general rule of thumb, you should use images that are easy to delineate and separate into different sections. Images where everything blends together are sometimes hard to use because visitors can't tell the difference between the various clickable sections (for example, Picasso paintings make terrible image maps).

For this example, I'm going to use a simple image that I created from scratch (see fig. 9.5). Once you've selected an image, you're ready to go on to the next step. This sample image is ideal because it's extremely easy to identify the different parts of the image and which HTML files they are linked to.

Fig. 9.5
A simple image map that might work for the top of my home page.

Mapping the Image Coordinates

Once you've chosen your image, the next step is to create a separate text file which tells your Web server how to interpret the clicks on various parts of the image. This file, called a map definition file, defines different areas on your image.

> **Note**
>
> This sort of program is usually used for creating map definition files for server-side image maps. The map definition file is actually just a plain ASCII text file, so we can use it for our purposes. We're just going to peek at it for the numbers. It's much easier than guessing—trust me.

As you learned in Chapter 6, when you set the height and width of images on your page, images are measured in pixels, or dots displayed on your screen. (A standard VGA monitor is 640 pixels wide and 480 pixels high.) In your map definition file, the different clickable areas are specified by their pixel coordinates.

> **Tip**
>
> The pixel number system for every image begins at 0,0, which represents the upper left corner of the image. Numbers steadily increase as you move right and down on the image.

On the CD

On the CD, I've included several image map utilities that will create your map file automatically. My favorite is Map This!. Using Map This!, you can use your mouse to draw and link the different clickable areas of your image. You can find Map This! in the \HOMEPAGE\IMAGEMAP\MAPTHIS subdirectory on the CD-ROM.

> **Note**
>
> You can install Map This! onto your computer by copying it to your hard drive, or just run it directly from the home page CD.

Once you've started Map This!, choose File, New to bring up the Make New Image Map dialog box. Choose Lets Go Find One to bring up a file box that searches your hard drive for GIF and JPEG files. Find your image file and click the OK button to bring up the image in Map This! (see fig. 9.6).

Fig. 9.6
Here's my file ready
to be made into an
image map.

On your image, you can define several different clickable shapes, including circles, squares, and polygons (refer to fig. 9.4). Using Map This!, you actually draw these shapes directly onto your image and link them to separate HTML files. Click the icon of the shape you want to draw and then actually draw on your image. Each clickable area you define is surrounded by a very light dotted line, as shown in figure 9.7.

Tip

When developing Web pages, remember to KISS (Keep it Simple, Stupid). The more complex your shapes, the more work—in the form of typing—you're going to create for yourself when it comes time to enter the client-side data into your HTML document.

Fig. 9.7
I have three rectangu-
lar shapes defined on
my sample image.

Once your shapes are drawn, you've got to tell Map This! the URL of the HTML file you want each piece to link to. Click the Select Existing Area icon (the little arrow) and click a clickable area. Now click the Edit Selected Area Info icon (the pencil) to bring up the settings for that clickable region (see fig. 9.8).

Tip

The last shape you draw should be a rectangle that covers the entire area of your image. Drag that rectangle from the top left corner of your image all the way to the bottom right corner. We'll use this later to create our "default" area.

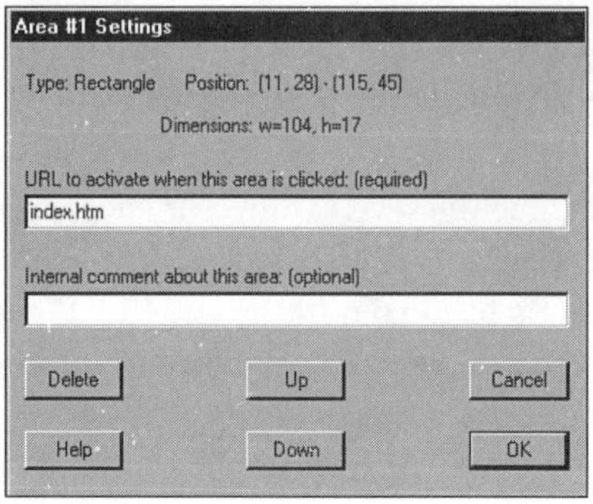

Fig. 9.8
Notice the pixel coordinates in the top of this box.

Type in the URL of the HTML file you want to load. To load a file that is in the same directory as the page this image is on, you only need to type in the filename.

When you are finished, choose File, Save from the menu to bring up the Info About This Mapfile dialog box (see fig. 9.9).

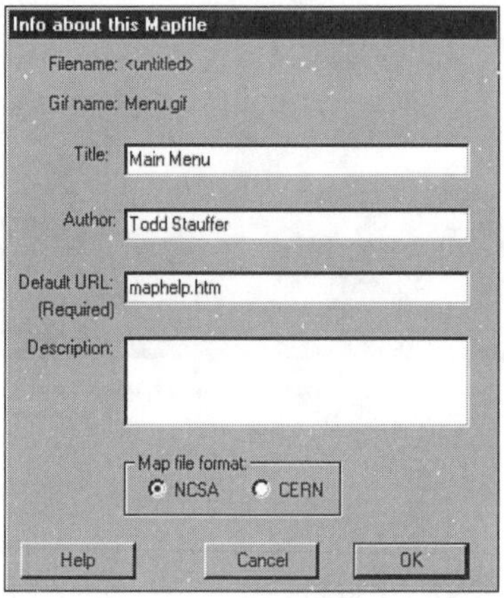

Fig. 9.9
Type important info about your image map in this dialog box.

From here, type a description and title of the image map file, if you want. Also make sure you choose NCSA as your map definition type.

Click OK and you'll then be prompted for a filename (mine is named `menu.txt`). Now we just need to understand the relevant data out of the map definition file. Here's what's significant in my file:

```
rect index.htm            11,28 115,45
rect books.htm            11,96 115,114
rect contract.htm         11,128 115,145
circle about.htm          301,42 329,67
circle resume.htm         300,126 329,152
circle maphelp.htm        0,0 345,165
```

Take a quick look at your map definition file (remember, it's a text file, so you can open it in Notepad) and make sure you can see information like this. You'll need this info to create the client-side clickable shapes in a moment.

Adding the Image to Your Home Page

Now you need to add the image map to your page. The only difference between this and a regular image is that you need to add the USEMAP attribute to your <IMG> tag. This attribute tells the browser to remember where the user clicked the image, and then look up those coordinates in the map definition data.

Here's the HTML that I use to add the example we've just created:

```
<IMG SRC="menu.gif" USEMAP="#menumap">
```

All that's new here is the USEMAP attribute; notice that it works a lot like the target links we talked about in Chapter 7. You need a # sign and a name for the USEMAP attribute. You'll use that same name later for the map definition data.

While we're here, there's one other thing you can do with your image map that makes it work in any graphical browser on the market today. What is it? Wrap it in a hypertext link. That link loads a "help" page that explains to users that they just clicked an image map, but the browser doesn't support them. For instance:

```
<A HREF="help.htm">
<IMG SRC="menu.gif" USEMAP="#menumap">
</A>
```

The USEMAP attribute is only recognized by Spyglass-compatible browsers that know how to deal with client-side maps. So, other browsers will just think you made a mistake and ignore it. In that case, this will work exactly like a normal clickable graphic.

> **Tip**
>
> Your help page should probably also offer your user another way to get at your site—like a bulleted list of links, for example.

You may be ahead of me on this one, but there's actually one other thing you can do to make this image map work better for text-based browsers, too. How? Add ALT text, like in the following example:

```
<A HREF="help.htm">
<IMG SRC="menu.gif" ALT="Main Menu" USEMAP="#menumap">
</A>
```

By adding ALT text to your <IMG> tag, you make it possible for text-based browsers to see this link and at least get to the help page. From there, text-based users can access the same basic links that your other non-Netscape/Internet Explorer users have available.

Adding the Image Map Data

Now all you have left is a little typing. The final step is adding the data you gathered in the map definition file to your HTML document. You do that with two new tags—the <MAP> and <AREA> tags.

The <MAP> tag will look something like this:

```
<MAP NAME="menumap">
</MAP>
```

The name for <MAP>'s NAME attribute needs to be the exact same name used in the USEMAP attribute that references this data, except that it doesn't include the # sign.

> **Note**
>
> The <MAP> information has to be in the <BODY> section of the current HTML document, but that's the only rule. You can put it at the very end (or beginning) of the <BODY> section, if you like.

Now you need to actually add the map definition data. With the map definition file in hand (or on-screen, as the case may be), you can begin to enter the data for your client-side map. Here's the format:

```
<MAP NAME="menumap">
<AREA SHAPE="RECT" COORDS="x,y,..." HREF="about.htm">
<AREA SHAPE="RECT" COORDS="x,y,..." HREF="books.htm">
<AREA SHAPE="RECT" COORDS="x,y,"    HREF="resume.htm">
</MAP>
```

Each <AREA> tag defines the shapes you created using the map definition program (like Map This!). The coordinates can be entered exactly as they are in the map definition file. For rectangles, you're simply defining the top left and bottom right corners.

Tip

The HREF attribute to <AREA> can just as easily accept target links if you'd like to use the image map to reference sections of the current page.

Area Shapes

The shapes and coordinates for client-side maps aren't remarkably different from those created by your map definition program, but you might want to see how these things work for yourself. (You don't have to use a map definition program, after all. If you can think in pixels, just eyeball it!)

Table 9.1 shows you how coordinates work for each shape.

Table 9.1   Shapes for Client-Side Maps

Shape	<AREA> Name	Coordinates
Rectangle	RECT	(top left) x,y, (bottom right) x,y
Circle	CIRCLE	(center) x, (center) y, (radius) n
Polygon	POLY	x,y,x1,y1,x2,y2

(I never in my life thought I'd write something that looks so much like algebra.) I guess that table needs some explanation. I've already said that a RECT takes the x and y coordinates for both the top left and bottom right corners. A CIRCLE needs both x and y coordinates for its center point; then it needs a number (in pixels) for the radius of the circle. Since a POLY polygon can have as many as 100 sides, you can enter up to 99 difference sets of x and y coordinates to define the points in that polygon.

III

Spicing Up Your Web Page

> **Note**
>
> To use the map definition file data for our client-side map, we'll need to do a little computing of our own, if only for the CIRCLE shape. Here's an example of the data I got for a circle in my map definition file:
>
> ```
> circle about.htm       301,42 329,67
> ```
>
> The problem with this data is that we don't need two points—we need a center point and a radius. How do we get them? Easy.
>
> The first set of coordinates (301,42) is the center point of the circle. To get the radius, ignore the y value of the second point. The x value is 329, which is on the edge of our circle. 329 – 301 = 28. Since 301 is the center's x and 329 is an x on the edge, then the difference, 28, is the radius for that circle.

So what good is a polygon? Consider this <AREA> tag:

```
<AREA SHAPE="POLY" COORDS="0,10,5,0,10,10" HREF="mypage.htm">
```

Using the POLY shape, you can create nearly anything—like this triangle. With coordinates at 0,10 and 5,0 and 10,10, we've got a nice little triangle.

The Default *<AREA>*

The last thing we need to talk about before putting this whole thing together is the default link for your <MAP> definition data. You may have noticed that the map definition file you created has a DEFAULT section as part of the file. In client-side maps, we don't have a DEFAULT shape, as such, so we have to fake it.

Fortunately, there's a handy little rule. When in doubt, the <AREA> tag that appears first in your <MAP> data takes precedence. That means that any overlap between <AREA> shapes will automatically reference the shape that was created first.

What that means is that we can create an <AREA> shape for the *entire* graphic, and place it last. That way, any part of the image map that isn't covered in a particular shape's definition still produces a result—in fact, it should probably point the user to a page that helps them figure out how to use image maps!

Here's an example:

```
<AREA SHAPE="RECT" COORDS="0,0,50,50" HREF="maphelp.htm">
```

As long as I put this default shape at the very end of my <MAP> definition, I'm okay.

The Finished Client-Side Map

Putting it all together, my example client-side map has added all this to the HTML document:

```
<A HREF="help.htm">
<IMG SRC="menu.gif" ALT="Main Menu" USEMAP="#menumap">
</A>
```

Other HTML includes the following:

```
<MAP NAME="menumap">
<AREA SHAPE="RECT" COORDS="11,28,115,45" HREF="index.htm">
<AREA SHAPE="RECT" COORDS="11,96,115,114" HREF="books.htm">
<AREA SHAPE="RECT" COORDS="11,128,115,145" HREF="contract.htm">
<AREA SHAPE="CIRCLE" COORDS="301,42,28" HREF="about.htm">
<AREA SHAPE="CIRCLE" COORDS="300,126,29" HREF="resume.htm">
<AREA SHAPE="RECT" COORDS="0,0,345,165" HREF="maphelp.htm">
</MAP>
```

You see where this can get complicated. Using a program like Map This! really helps. Figure 9.10 shows you how this looks in Internet Explorer.

> **Tip**
>
> The data you got from Map This! isn't gospel; it's just a guideline. Notice, for instance, that one of my circles has a center at x = 301 and the other's center is at x = 300. There's nothing wrong with changing one of those two values so they're the same, if that level of accuracy is desired.

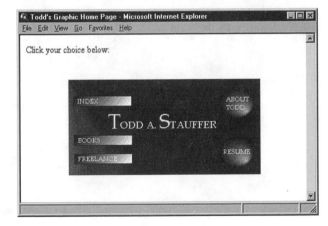

Fig. 9.10
This client-side map gives my Web site a completely new interface to make maneuvering easier for users.

CHAPTER 10

Making Your Web Page Multimedia

Imagine making the movie *Star Wars*. All George Lucas started with was a plain old text manuscript (which you can download at **http://www.books.com**). That manuscript may have been thorough, but it wasn't nearly as much fun as the actual movie. You needed the great soundtrack and cool special effects to make the movie fun and enjoyable. Without them, *Star Wars* would have been just like any other typical movie about intergalactic war.

While we aren't going to create *Star Wars*, you will learn how you can add all sorts of special effects to your home page. Adding audio bites and sound clips is within your reach, and they'll separate your page from all the other text/image-only pages out there.

So far, I've only showed you how you can mark your own corner of the Internet quickly and easily with a simple Web page. Now it's time to go that extra step and make your home page truly spectacular. You'll learn how to integrate audio bites and video clips onto your Web page to create a truly multimedia effect.

A Sampling of Multimedia Sites

Before I show you how to use these new multimedia formats on your own pages, let's take a look at how some other multimedia Web pages are set up. Several places on the Web integrate text, images, audio, and video clips on the same page to achieve startlingly good effects—and then there are those pages that you don't want your page to look like.

Using all of these different media types presents several technical and design challenges. All of the design issues that came up when adding images to pages are now back, in threefold. You've got to worry about making these new aspects easy to use and have them naturally appear in your page, without adding too much clutter and making your page unreadable.

On the technical side, creating and adding audio and video clips is no walk in the park. You've got to worry about file size, multi-platform compatibility (will PC, Mac, and UNIX users all be able to use the clips?), and the quality of the clip.

The CNN Video Vault

Here's one way to add multimedia to your site—make it a separate page altogether! Of course, CNN has the resources to put together a serious archive in the Video Vault (**http://www.cnn.com/video_vault/index.html**) for its many users to peruse (see fig. 10.1). But notice that CNN has included just a simple HTML list of the movies available, and it tells you how large each movie file is. It's also gone with QuickTime movies which is easily among the most cross-platform movie formats. (MPEG would also be good.)

Fig. 10.1
Simple and easy to use, this site is a model for a basic page that gives you multimedia access.

The NASA Shuttle Site

Head straight to this site for up-to-the-minute information on the latest Space Shuttle mission, including photos, sounds, images, and real-time displays.

If you're ever curious to know what's going to happen next with the Shuttle, just point your browser to **http://shuttle.nasa.gov/** and you're guaranteed to get lost for a few hours (see fig. 10.2).

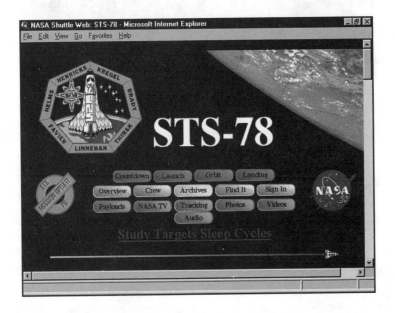

Fig. 10.2
Almost everything you could ever want to know about the Space Shuttle is available in full-blown multimedia.

Aside from the basic information about the Shuttle's departure, payload, mission, and achievements, you can even see still images of NASA TV while listening to the live broadcast with the RealAudio helper application (or Netscape compatible plug-in). Go one further, and you can use CU-See Me technology to watch NASA TV live over the Net!

Star Trek Voyager

Another one of my favorite true multimedia sites is the Star Trek Voyager home page (**http://voyager.paramount.com/VoyagerActive.html**). This professionally designed page demonstrates what a lot of time and effort can accomplish. Even if you're really not much of a trekkie, there are so many neat images, sounds, and video clips available on this site that it's worth stopping by for a look (see fig. 10.3).

Fig. 10.3
Multimedia pages don't get much better than this. Crisp, clear instructions let you know exactly how to experience all the audio and video features.

Understanding and Using Audio Clips

Audio clips, sometimes referred to as sound bites, add another dimension to your page. Not only can people see information you present, but they can hear it as well. Imagine watching *Raiders of the Lost Ark* without hearing the theme music—it just wouldn't be the same. Sound is a welcome addition to home pages because it makes them a lot more fun to explore.

Unlike adding images, when you put an audio clip on your home page, you are linking to an actual file that must be downloaded and played in separate steps. Images just appear alongside your text. Visitors who come to your home page choose which files to download and then subsequently play the audio clip on their computer.

> **Note**
>
> To hear audio clips on your computer, you need to have the correct hardware and software. If you are using a PC-compatible machine, you must have a sound card (preferably SoundBlaster or compatible) and speakers hooked up. Most multimedia kits that come with CD-ROM drives include all the necessary hardware to hear sound clips. PC users also need audio software to actually hear their files being played. You can find a handful of audio players on the CD-ROM included with this book. Macintosh users, on the other hand, have it even easier. Their multimedia capabilities are built-in.

In this section, I'll outline the different types of audio file formats and tell you where you can find your own audio clips to add to your home page.

Explaining Audio File Types and Formats

On the Web, you'll see a wide variety of audio clip file types and formats. These formats represent the different methods used to electronically record the sounds with a computer. They all have their own advantages and common uses.

Choosing from the different sound file types is like picking the speed of film for your camera. For a 35mm camera, you can choose speeds like 100, 200, 400, or 1,000, depending on the lighting and other factors that could affect the quality of your images.

Likewise, there are three audio file formats to be familiar with (see Table 10.1).

Table 10.1	Common Audio File Formats
Format	**Description**
.AU	Developed by Sun, this file format is called *mu-law*, and uses 8-bit sampling which makes the sounds crackle (like using a cordless phone), but offers reasonably acceptable quality. Recently, an 11-bit version of the .AU audio format has started becoming more popular because it provides better quality. .AU files tend to be small, compact, easy to download, and work on all types of computers. This file type is the 200-speed 35mm film of the computer sound world. It's an international standard and works on just about every type of computer you can imagine.
.WAV	This is the Microsoft Windows audio format. The .WAV extension is used for audio files created for use primarily under Microsoft Windows. While .WAV files tend to be of higher quality than the .AU format (and have significantly larger file size), there can be some problems with listening to them on different types of computers.
.AIFF	This is the Macintosh audio file format. Not very common on the Web, .AIFF has the same limitations .WAV has for multi-computer compatibility.

On the CD

The included CD comes with programs that let you record and listen to any of these three file types, preparing you for virtually anything you'll find on the Web. See Appendix B, "Home Page Final Checklist," for more information.

> **Tip**
>
> If you want to know more technical details about the audio file formats listed in Table 10.1 (such as what 8-bit sampling really is), I would recommend reading the Audio File Format FAQ (Frequently Asked Questions) which can be found on the WWW at **http://www.cis.ohio-state.edu/hypertext/faq/usenet/audio-fmts/ top.html**.

Where You Can Find Audio Clips

Now that you're familiar with the different types of audio clips, you'll probably want to add some to your home page. There are several different ways for you to obtain innovative and creative audio clips. Most people browse the WWW until they find audio clips that they like; others purchase the necessary equipment and digitize their own.

Included on the CD-ROM in the back of the book, you'll find several different sample audio files, in both AU and WAV formats. These audio files are meant to be a sampling of the kind you'll put on your home page.

On the CD

> **Tip**
>
> Feel free to use the included AU and WAV audio clips on your home page however you like. You'll find a wide variety in the /AUDIO subdirectory on the CD-ROM.

Finding Audio Clips on the Internet

The Internet is a fantastic resource for music and audio clips of all sorts. You can download everything from Jim Carrey's rantings ("Allllrighty then") to Martin Luther King's "I Have a Dream" speech. Below, I've compiled a diverse list of popular WWW sites where you can find, download, and listen to audio clips. These are public archives that allow anyone to download their files:

- **http://sunsite.unc.edu/pub/multimedia/sun-sounds/ movies/**—This site has a fantastic set of movie sound clips from practically every movie you can remember. Some examples include snippets from *Blade Runner*, *Aliens*, and *The Raiders of the Lost Ark*.

- **http://parkhere.com/tvbytes**—This is the most complete TV theme song site I have ever seen. If the show even had a pilot episode, you can find its theme song here. Stop by here to find everything from *Mission Impossible* to *60 Minutes*.

- **http://Web.msu.edu/vincent/index.html**—Famous people and speeches can be found here. I found Martin Luther King's "I Have a Dream" speech on this site.

- **http://www.acm.uiuc.edu/rml/**—This is the most complete spot for digital audio and video clips that I could find. The site includes links to hundreds of different multimedia sites around the Web—a great place to explore!

Make Your Own Audio Clips

Finding neat audio clips on the WWW is fine for some people, but most of us want to have our own customized audio clips for our home page. Creating your own audio clips isn't too difficult or costly—it just requires a little bit of know-how.

Macintosh users have it easy. Nowadays, Macs come with multimedia capabilities and even their own microphones and software. You can speak directly to your Macintosh, have it record your speech, and put it on your home page within a few minutes. Make sure you save your audio file format in the AU file format (instead of Mac's AIFF format)—AU is the most popular format on the WWW.

Don't fret if you are a PC owner though. Practically anyone who has a CD-ROM multimedia kit can create their own audio files nearly as easily. You can buy a cheap microphone (the Microsoft Sound System Kit comes with all the recording software and a microphone for under $50) to digitize your voice. For more advanced clips, you can connect your stereo directly into your sound card with a standard RCA cable.

Caution

Make sure you don't record sounds that you don't own. For example, you may really like the new U2 album, but digitizing it and making it available on your home page is illegal and could get you into hot water.

Note

I've just glossed over the process of recording your own audio clips here. Make sure you consult your system and multimedia manuals to learn how to digitize sounds properly on your specific computer. If you have trouble digitizing in AU format, the sound programs included on the book's CD-ROM will convert practically any sound format into the AU format.

III

Spicing Up Your Web Page

Adding Audio Clips to Your Home Page

Actually, the hardest part of putting an audio clip on your home page is obtaining the right clip. Once you have an audio clip in hand, adding it to your home page is a breeze. You use the same HTML tags as you used to insert a link into your page, <A HREF=> and </A>.

Let's say I wanted to add an audio welcome to visitors who stop by my page for the first time. After recording the greeting, I saved the file as GREETING.AU. To add it to my home page, I simply type the following lines of HTML:

```
<A HREF="GREETING.AU">Welcome from Todd (130K) </A>
```

This line is an actual HTML link to my sound file. Instead of playing or trying to display GREETING.AU in the actual browser program, a separate audio player will load and play the message when it is clicked.

It's also often a good idea to call out your audio files with a picture or an icon that helps it make sense. For instance:

```
<A HREF="GREETING.AU">
<IMG SRC="sound.gif">
Welcome from Todd (130K)
</A>
```

As usual, that could all be on one line in HotDog if we wanted it to be, but I've added the line returns for clarity. Notice that I've added an icon inside the link tags, so that both the icon and text are clickable (see fig.10.4).

Fig. 10.4

Now anyone can hear my voice!

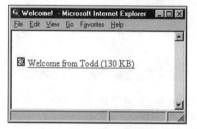

Note

Did you notice how I put the audio file size in parenthesis? That's so visitors to my Web page can estimate how long it will take to download the sound clip before they click the link. As a common courtesy, you should list the file size of every audio and video file that you add to your home page.

Understanding and Using Video Clips

Video clips are combinations of movie pictures and sound bundled up together just like a movie. You can find video clips ranging from snippets of actual films to celebrity interviews. The range of video clips available is vast, though not nearly as large as the number of images and audio sounds available. Like adding audio clips to your home page, video clips are not played directly in the user's browser. Home page visitors must download the clip and run a separate program to display the video clip on their computer.

Unfortunately, video clips have several drawbacks that can make them difficult to use. The main problem is file size. Video clips are gigantic, usually 1-2 megs in file size. That's because a video clip is a conglomeration of hundreds of images set to display one after another in rapid succession. Remember how I talked about image size in Chapter 5? A one-minute, TV-quality video clip can have as many as 1,800 different image frames.

Downloading a 2 meg file at the fastest speed your computer probably supports (28.8 baud) and in ideal conditions will still take 10–20 minutes. For the millions of WWW users using 14.4 or slower baud modems, the large file size often means that they won't spend the time downloading the video clip.

Note

Don't forget that you've only got 2 MB of space to work with on AOL. One large video clip could easily take up that amount of space. Of course, that 2 MB limit is per screen name, so you might want to create additional screen names and store your video file in the My Place directory for a secondary screen name. You can then link to it using its full URL.

Explaining Video File Types and Formats

There are several different types of video clips that you may run across when browsing on the Web. Currently, none of them reign supreme as the default video standard, so you have to decide which of the popular formats you want to use in your home page.

Primarily, there are three video file formats to be familiar with (see Table 10.2).

Table 10.2 Common Video File Formats	
Format	**Description**
MPEG (.MPG)	One of the oldest video formats around, MPEG is similar to the JPEG image file format, only optimized for videos. The MPEG format is popular because video clips in this format tend to be of decent quality. Unfortunately, the MPEG format is hardware intensive and needs a lot of RAM and special hardware to create. You'll have to buy a special piece of equipment used to encode videos (in most cases), and make sure you've got at least 16 megs of RAM.
AVI (.AVI)	Similar to the .WAV audio style, this is Microsoft's Video for Windows file format. Windows users can use AVI video files easily because they are optimized to be seen on a Windows computer. This video format is less popular than the other two, but still commonly used.
QT (.QT/.MOV)	QT, or QuickTime, is the video format developed and licensed by Apple Computer. Taking the Web by storm, most new video clips are released in QuickTime format because it is multi-platform, has a compact file size, and is easier to record with. My recommendation is to stick with the QuickTime format.

On the CD

The included CD comes with programs that let you watch virtually any type of video or animation clip that you'll find on the Web. See Appendix C, "Home Page Final Checklist," for more information.

Tip

If you want to know more technical details about the video formats listed in Table 10.2, try the following links:

- MPEG—**http://www.cis.ohio-state.edu/hypertext/faq/usenet/mpeg-faq/top.html**
- AVI—**http://www.microsoft.com/kb/**
- QT—**http://www.QuickTimeFAQ.org/**

Where You Can Find Video Clips

The same obstacle that presented itself when adding audio to your home page comes back for video clips. Finding high-quality and useful video clips that you want to add to your home page can be an extremely difficult task.

On the CD

Included on the CD-ROM, you'll find several different sample video clips in QT format. Take a look at how they work to get an idea of what kind of video clips you can use in your home page. The video clips are in the /VIDEO/ subdirectory on the CD-ROM.

Finding Video Clips on the Internet

There are several different WWW sites that have large collections of MPEG and QT movies. Downloading them all could take several weeks, but it's not a bad idea to stop by and pick up a few fun clips.

Here's a partial list of some hot spots to find good MPEG and QT files on the Web:

- **http://w3.eeb.ele.tue.nl/mpeg/index.html**—A fantastic collection of movies in several different categories can be found here. Their video clips range from repairing the Hubble telescope to episodes of *The Simpsons* (quite a variety).

- **http://www.acm.uiuc.edu/rml/**—This is the most complete spot for digital audio and video clips that I could find. As I mentioned previously (in the audio clip section), this page has links to popular multimedia sites all over the WWW.

- **http://deathstar.rutgers.edu/people/bochkay/movies.html**—An ever growing variety of QuickTime movies. You'll find different video clips that contain Kathy Ireland, Barney the Dinosaur, and Star Trek here.

Make Your Own Video Clips

Just a year or two ago, if you had wanted to make your own video clips and put them on your home page, I would have strongly advised against it. At that point, the equipment required to digitize video and store it in electronic format was way too expensive and difficult to use.

Nowadays, it's a different story. You have several affordable low cost alternatives to creating your own video clips. Basic video cameras that connect directly to your computer come with hardware and software for under $200. You can also make video clips from VCR tapes that you already have. For about the same price range, you can purchase a digital converter, which lets your VCR and computer talk to each other.

Stop by your local computer store to learn more about your digitizing options. By the way, most of the affordable software digitizes video into QuickTime format.

III

Spicing Up Your Web Page

Adding Video Clips to Your Pages

Video clips are just as easy to add to your home page as an audio clip is. You use the exact same tag, only you specify the video's filename instead.

It's about as simple as the following:

```
<IMG SRC="video.gif">
<A HREF="WELCOME.QT">Welcome to my site (1.3 Meg)</A>
```

The first line inserts a miniature video icon which tells visitors that the link next to it is a video clip. It's not required for the link to work, and, as with the sound link earlier in this chapter, you could easily include the icon between the link tags to make it clickable. The second line is an actual HTML link to my video clip. When clicked, visitors will download the QuickTime video clip, load a video player for their computer, and watch the clip automatically (see fig. 10.5).

Tip

Instead of a simple video icon, it's a fairly common practice to use a still image from the video itself as a "thumbnail" clickable image for a video link.

Fig. 10.5
A video clip in action.

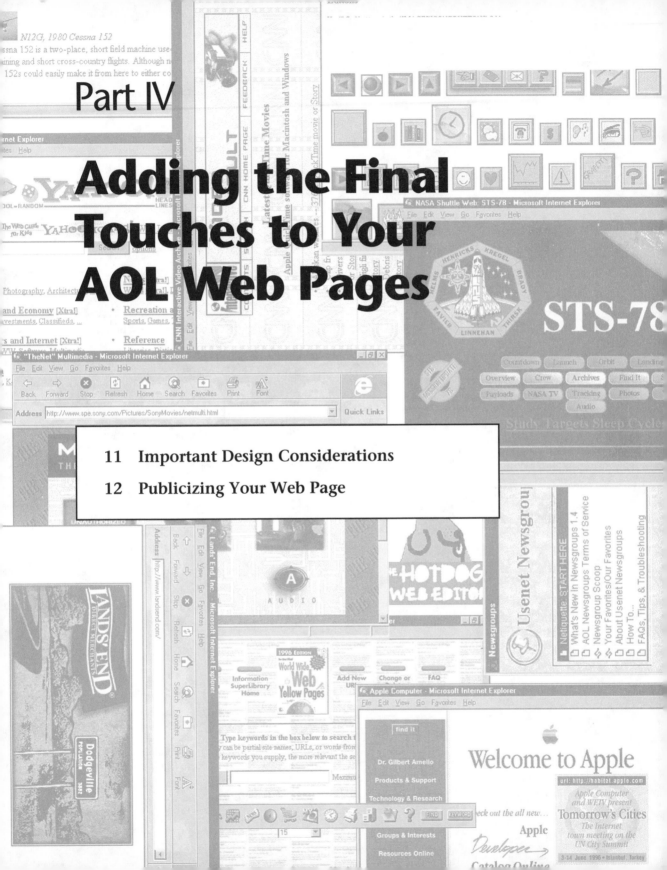

Part IV

Adding the Final Touches to Your AOL Web Pages

CHAPTER 11

Important Design Considerations

After reading ten chapters, you've made it through all the HTML tags, links, and images for creating a decent-looking home page. This section teaches you how to put the final touches on your page before you make it available for millions of WWW surfers to see.

So far, I've mentioned many different tips and tricks for creating a high-quality Web page. This chapter helps you put all those tips together. You've already put your page together, for the most part. Now we just need to go back over it with the eagle-eye of a good copy editor.

Home Page Design Tips

As you've learned in this book, you can create a home page in just a matter of minutes. HotDog helps you decipher complicated HTML tags with ease and lets you add new elements with your mouse. However, while creating a basic home page isn't too difficult, there are several things you should keep in mind when designing how your page looks. In this section, I'll go over a couple of popular (but simple) design tips that will help your Web pages look great.

Measure Your Page's Consistency

All telephones work the same. You pick up the receiver and start dialing the person you want to reach. When you're done, you hang up the receiver to stop your conversation. Sure, some phones require a special number to be dialed (like 9) to work, and others hide their buttons in hard-to-find spots, but all of them generally work the same. This consistency is what lets you know how to use a phone from anywhere in the world.

Visitors to your Web site appreciate that same type of consistency on your home page. All your Web pages should have a consistent style about them. Soon, visitors will know where to find that information on your Web pages without hunting for it.

Some examples of consistency are the following:

- Use the same headline format on every Web page. If you use the <H1> tag to label your home page, then you should use an <H1> tag to label every page in your site. Using different-sized headlines on different pages will look odd.

- Add graphics and images in similar ways throughout your home page. If some of your graphics link to other Web sites, and others don't, visitors might not recognize which graphics are which and could get confused.

- Include the same information in each page's footer. At the bottom of every Web page, you include important information about when it was created and who to contact for further information. Add this same default footer to every page in your site.

Brevity is a Virtue

Some people like to compare the World Wide Web to a book that people can read and jump around from page to page. I prefer to liken the Web to a glossy magazine—one where people flip through the pages randomly. Every now and then a story or headline might catch their eye but, for the most part, pages are being flipped about as fast as their hand can move. With a short reader attention span, magazines have to present information that is concise, clear, and useful.

With this in mind, it's a good idea to keep your Web pages brief and uncluttered. Using a mouse, people browse through Web pages quickly. If something looks long and boring to read, they keep going until they see something that catches their eye. Think of your own browsing techniques. It's easy to run out of patience when browsing the WWW. If there is too much information, or something doesn't jump out and grab you, you're more likely to jump to another page before slowly reading and digesting several paragraphs of text. Figure 11.1 shows you what a home page looks like when it has too much text on it.

If you really have a lot of information to put on your home page, consider splitting the information up onto several different pages (see "Expanding Your Home Page into a Home Site" in Chapter 8) and letting visitors link to the various pieces they want to read. This keeps them from becoming over-loaded with information.

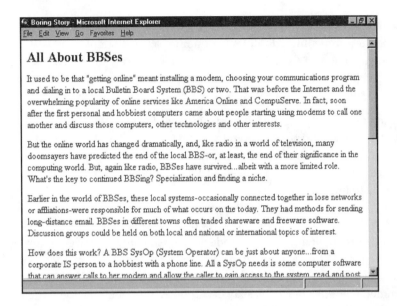

Fig. 11.1
Nobody will
bother reading
this; it's boring.

To keep my readers interested (while keeping my home page brief), I use a simple rule of thumb that I call the three-by-three rule. Basically, the three-by-three rule tells me to not ever place more than three paragraphs (each with three sentences) together on a home page. After three paragraphs, readers become bored and move on. Instead, I use lists and tables to bring out important information and catch visitors' eyes.

> **Tip**
>
> Also keep in mind that every person who visits your home page must download everything that's on it (including all the text and pictures) before reading it. The smaller your page, the less time people spend waiting, twiddling their thumbs, for your home page to download. Remember that text downloads much faster than images. An entire page of text can download, at times, more quickly than a single image.

Of course, rules are made to be broken, and I've come across some very interesting sites that were text heavy—especially if the site was put together by a good writer. If you've got a little fiction to get across on your Web site, or a very amusing account of a vacation you've take, go ahead and type away.

Just keep the copy clean with paragraph breaks, tasteful graphics or icons, and the occasional horizontal line.

Don't Overdo Your Web Page with Glitz

Along these same lines, don't let your home page get out of hand with too much glamour and glitz. Everyone knows that you can add lots of pictures, sound clips, cool forms, and clickable maps to your home page; just don't overuse these HTML gimmicks.

When your home page uses so many different features all at once, it becomes difficult to read and hard to even look at. Don't try to add every neat HTML feature and trick you can think of to the same page. Although it's an impressive display of WWW knowledge and ability, it'll be gaudy to look at and impossible to understand.

Keep Your Home Page Alive

Every Thursday night, a new episode of Seinfeld comes on. Every week, when you turn the TV on, you know that you aren't going to see the same episode you watched last time because that would be boring. Except for during the summer, new episodes are weekly occurrences. Can you imagine if there were only one episode, and NBC played it over and over again? You'd watch it the first time, and maybe see the rerun once, but after that, you'd switch channels. The reason you keep coming back Thursday at 9:00 is because you know you'll see something new.

You should practice this same philosophy on your home page. If you create a basic page and never update it or make changes, why would anyone come back? After one or two stops, they've seen everything there is to see on your home page and will start visiting other WWW spots instead.

The key to getting visitors to come back again and again is to constantly update your pages to keep information fresh and new. One great example of a constantly updating site is the Weather Channel's home page at **http:// www.weather.com/** (see fig. 11.2). Every time you visit, you can get current weather maps and information.

Once you've built a basic home page, keeping it fresh, new, and exciting is difficult, but well worth the trouble. For example, lawyers might keep a list of links relating to landmark precedents and decisions that their clients might be interested in. Accountants might note recent tax changes, and offer regular tips on how to prepare for April 15th.

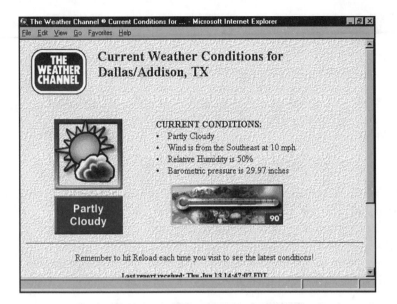

Fig. 11.2
Can you imagine
if this page was
never updated?

Improving Your HTML Code

One of the most common problems that I notice with Web pages is something most people wouldn't think about. I'm referring to how the HTML text (called *source files*) appears when you look at it as a straight "source" document (in HotDog, or any other text editor). Why is this important? You might think it isn't, since you usually never even see the underlying HTML file unless you've created it.

While technically it doesn't matter what your HTML source file looks like, you'll find that it makes a big difference when you try updating and making changes to your home page in the future. It doesn't take much time, or effort, to structure your HTML source file properly. You won't immediately reap many benefits from these few suggested improvements, but you'll be glad you did for future updates.

In six months, you may not remember why you used a table instead of a list to display your personal information. Or, even worse, you'll spend six hours trying to decipher your cryptic HTML tags. The more complex your pages become, the more effort you'll have to put into updating the files—if only because the straight HTML codes are difficulty to read.

That's why you should add comments to your home page. Comments never appear in in the user's browser; they only show up when you are reading your home page as a text file.

Note

In the world of computer programmers, these guidelines are strictly enforced as coding standards. That's because different people often work on the same program. So, everyone has to follow the same formatting standards to make sure their work is readable. While no one else may be looking over your shoulder and grading your home page, following these guidelines is highly recommended for formatting your HTML source code.

Make It Readable

The easiest hint for readable HTML documents is to add tabs and returns. They don't affect the way the home page is laid out; the tags do that. Web browsers will ignore any and all tabs or returns. This means separating paragraphs of text, separating and making links easy to read, and lining up related information such as lists and tables.

Caution

There is one exception. Tabs and returns do affect text that appears between <PRE> tags. Make sure you don't accidentally add tabs and returns (or even extra spaces) if you're using <PRE> to format important text.

Take a look at figures 11.3 and 11.4. Both of them look exactly the same when displayed with Internet Explorer. In figure 11.3, the text is a confused, jumbled mess of text that is practically impossible to read. Just a simple use of tabs, returns, and spaces (shown in figure 11.4) cleans up that mess. Which would you rather work with?

Your goal is to make your HTML file as readable as possible. Don't be afraid to use the tab or spacebar to line items up or to use the Enter key to separate paragraphs of text.

Tip

One popular way of formatting your source code is by typing your HTML tags in all caps. This makes the tags stand out and easier to notice when you quickly scan a document. Browsers generally aren't case-sensitive when it comes to tags, so most don't care if an <HMTL> tag looks like <html>, <Html>, or <hTmL>.

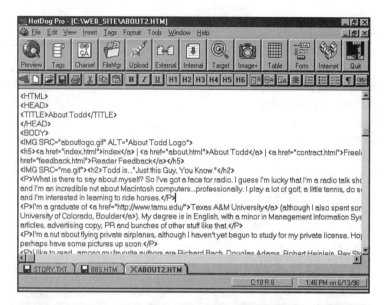

Fig. 11.3
HTML formatted
like this is not fun,
nor easy to update.

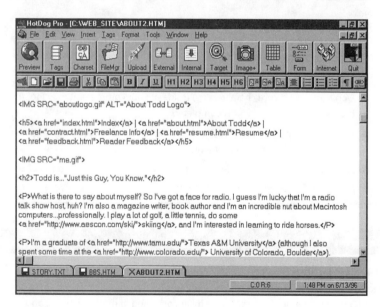

Fig. 11.4
This is a better
example of a well-
formatted HTML
document.

Comment Your HTML

Another popular way to enhance your HTML source code is by adding comments. *Comments* are specially marked sentences and phrases that never appear in the browser window, but are part of the HTML source code. In your

HTML source code, comments are surrounded by `<!--` and `-->`, as in the following example:

```
<!-- Here's a sample comment -->
```

Comments are particularly useful for recording your thoughts or explaining complicated pieces of HTML code. For example, if you use an image map on your home page, you might want to include a comment that explains what choices the image map offers. Since you may not have the image handy when updating your source code later, this would be useful information to have available, as in the following HTML example:

```
<!-- This image map lets people choose their delivery type.
Truck > truck.html
Airplane > airplane.html
Ship > ship.html
See the image or MAP file for more information. -->
<A HREF="delivery.imp">
<IMG SRC="delivery.gif">
</A>
```

Note

Comments are a bit odd, as far as HTML tags go, and not every browser is as adept at reading them as are others. If you want to make sure that your HTML source file is browser-proof, then follow these few rules when commenting your source code:

- Don't use underscore characters (_) inside of your comment; it may fool the browser that the comment is completed.

- Place comments (`<!--` and `-->`) at the beginning and end of every line. Some browsers don't recognize comments that span multiple lines.

- Don't use other HTML tags inside of comments. This may cause other browsers to ignore the comment tags entirely.

Caution

Make sure you don't include private information in your home page comments because they can be read by anybody who visits your home page. Users can choose View, Source in Internet Explorer (or a similar command in most browsers), and comments will appear along with the rest of the source code. Passwords, personal phone numbers, and inappropriate language and remarks are examples of bad comment information.

Test Your Web Page

Before you submit a business report or term paper, you probably give it one final run through. You break out the spell-checker and give it to friends to read before submitting it to your boss, your customers, or a professor. Even though you spent a lot of time creating the perfect report, you almost invariably found small errors and silly mistakes that could make you look bad—or at least sloppy.

Can your Web page make the grade? Before you put your home page on the WWW and start announcing it to millions of people to visit (that's next chapter), you want to run a final check on your home page as well. With an eye out for detail, you should check it over for common and easily prevented errors. This section shows you how to check your home page for mistakes and validate it according to HTML standards.

Preview Your Page

Using HotDog, you can preview your HTML document anytime you wish. All you've got to do is click the Preview button located at the top of the HotDog screen. Internet Explorer loads up with the current HTML document automatically.

Take a good look at your home page. Here's a list of simple, but important, things to check when looking at your home page, and how to fix the problems:

- **Make sure your paragraphs are split up properly**—A common mistake is to forget the <P> tag between paragraphs. Without this tag, your paragraphs of text bunch together no matter how they appear in HotDog. If your paragraphs are too far apart using the <P> tag, try using <BR> instead. This tag doesn't add an extra space between paragraphs.

- **Confirm that images appear where they should**—When you start adding images to your home page, it is easy to use the wrong keywords (e.g., accidentally aligning an image on the right side of the screen instead of the left). Make sure your image is properly placed and sized on your home page and that text flows around the image correctly.

- **Check that all of your HTML tags are closed**—Another problem with home pages is forgetting or not closing a tag properly. On my About page shown in figure 11.5, I forgot to add the / to the </H1> closing tag at the top of my page. Oops. That one little mistake made quite a difference. Fortunately, you'll be using HotDog to add most of your tags, but you might change a tag accidentally.

Fig. 11.5
This page is not for
people who have
bad eyesight; it's
just a simple typo.

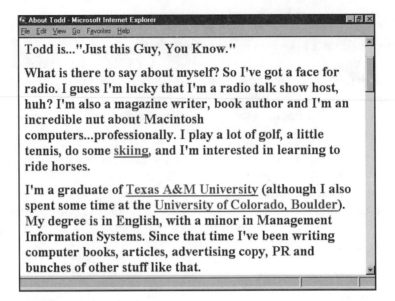

Todd is..."Just this Guy, You Know."

What is there to say about myself? So I've got a face for radio. I guess I'm lucky that I'm a radio talk show host, huh? I'm also a magazine writer, book author and I'm an incredible nut about Macintosh computers...professionally. I play a lot of golf, a little tennis, do some skiing, and I'm interested in learning to ride horses.

I'm a graduate of Texas A&M University (although I also spent some time at the University of Colorado, Boulder). My degree is in English, with a minor in Management Information Systems. Since that time I've been writing computer books, articles, advertising copy, PR and bunches of other stuff like that.

- **Test all of your links**—If you are going to include hypertext links on your page, make sure they work right, otherwise visitors often get an unfriendly screen that says the page is no longer available. A simple mistake, such as mistyping URLs, is easily avoided. Several tools exist that automatically check all of the links included in your home page. Try using the MOMSpider (**http://www.ics.uci.edu/WebSoft/ MOMspider/**) or Checker (**http://www.ugrad.cs.ubc.ca/spider/ q7f192/branch/win-checker.html**) to do this automatically.

- **Spell-check your page**—Spell-checking your page is probably one of the easiest and most effective ways of improving your page's appearance. Misspelled words signify that you didn't take the time necessary to check out your page. If you purchase HotDog Pro, you get a high-quality built in spell-checker. I just copy and paste text from Internet Explorer into Microsoft Word and run the Word spell-checker from there. It is cost-effective that way.

Tip

Notice that I cut and paste from Internet Explorer, not from HotDog. When you're viewing the page in IE, you can select all the text and drop it into a program that's capable of spell-checking, like a word processor. If you cut and paste from HotDog, you'll be spending a lot of time while the spell-checker asks you about all the HTML tags.

IV

The Final Touches

Use Another Browser

Although this book is geared for optimizing your home page for Internet Explorer and Netscape visitors, it's a good idea to check it out using another popular browser or two. Your home page may look fantastic in Internet Explorer, but be impossible to read for Mosaic users. You want it to be read by anyone on the WWW.

Both Internet Explorer and Netscape offer special tags that nearly no other browsers can deal with—and that's okay. At the same time, you should do everything you can to make sure that everyone can read your pages. Figure 11.6 shows my radio home page in AOL's pre-Internet Explorer Web browser.

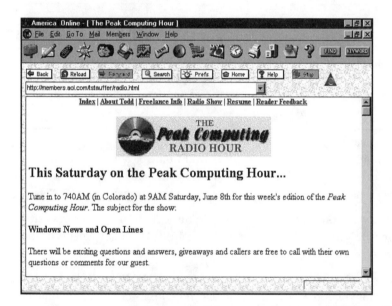

Fig. 11.6
Here's the older AOL browser displaying my page. It's important to check that it looks good here, as well as in Internet Explorer.

Tip

Older browsers typically don't support all of the new HTML and Netscape extensions. They may display items such as tables in a jumbled fashion. For example, older versions of AOL's browser don't recognize tables. Make sure you are always using the newest version of a WWW browser or AOL's access software.

Test and Validate Your HTML Document

After you've run through your HTML code with the previous checklist, you might be fairly well convinced that you've reached Web page perfection.

However, it's still worth your time running an HTML Validation Tool (created by the World Wide Web Consortium) over your home page. These tools look at your HTML source code and evaluate according to the official definition of how HTML should be used. Since HTML is a world wide standard, there is a very strict definition of how it is to be used, called a DTD (Document Type Definition)—it's the grammar-checker of the HTML world. You can take a look at the official HTML 2.0 standard at **http://www.w3.org/ hypertext/WWW/MarkUp/html-spec/html-pubtext.html**. You can find the HTML 3.2 standard at **http://www.w3.org/pub/WWW/ MarkUp/Wilbur/**.

Note

Netscape's and Microsoft's extensions work is above and beyond the official HTML definition, but those tags don't really interfere with the official definition. Stop by the Netscape home page (**http://www.netscape.com**) and the Internet Explorer home page (**http://www.microsoft.com/ie/**) for official information on their extensions.

The validation tools don't care what your home page looks like, how many links or graphics you include, or whether your paragraphs of information make sense. They only care whether or not you properly use HTML tags.

HTML validation tools are important because they ensure that your home page will be readable by browsers and cool WWW enhancements in the future.

For example, most browsers will interpret your HTML to the best of their ability. So, if you forgot to add the <HTML> and </HTML> tags to your home page, Netscape recognizes other HTML telltale signs and displays your document properly. A validation tool would recognize that you forgot the <HTML> tags and give you a reminder that your home page isn't official until it contains them.

In the future, other WWW tools might become available and not recognize your home page if it doesn't meet official HTML standards. So while an HTML validator may not improve the way your home page looks, it's an important tool for future compatibility.

HTML Validator

Let's check your home page with the easiest to use and most popular HTML validation service located at **http://www.webtechs.com/html-val-svc/** (see fig. 11.7). You tell the WebTechs Validation Service the URL of the document you want it to check, and it will link there automatically. Within a few moments, you'll know whether or not your home page meets HTML standards, and if not, what you can do to fix it.

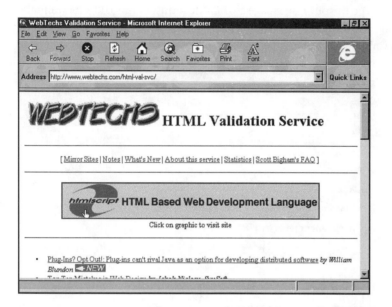

Fig. 11.7
The WebTechs Validation Service checks to see if you have written a technically correct home page.

> **Note**
>
> To validate your home page, it must first be available on the WWW, not your personal computer. The WebTechs Validation Service cannot evaluate HTML files on your local computer because it requires a valid URL to work properly. You'll need to upload the HTML document via the My Place area on AOL so that you can give WebTechs a valid URL.

The first step in validating your home page is selecting the level of HTML you want to use. The WebTechs Validation Service allows you to test the following number of different levels of HTML:

- Strict (compliant with only the recommended tags of HTML 2.0)
- Level 2 (the current standard)
- Level 3 (now-dead HTML 3.0)
- Level 3.2 (the current HTML 3.2 standard)
- Mozilla (the nickname for the Netscape extensions)
- Microsoft IE (Mozilla plus extra Microsoft extensions)

Since this book describes using all sorts of Netscape and IE enhancements to make your page look better, you might want to choose Microsoft IE in the WebTechs Validation Service screen. Then, in the Check Documents by URL box, type in your home page's URL. Click the Submit URLs for Validation button to validate your home page. Figure 11.8 shows the screen before I try to validate my home page.

Fig. 11.8

I'm getting ready to validate my home page.

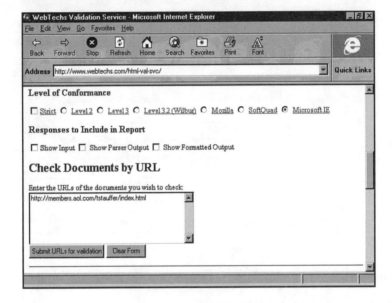

After clicking the button, the validation service fetches your home page and tests it for a variety of HTML faults and problems. If your home page fails the validation service, a screen appears that informs you why you have failed and helps you diagnose the problem. Once your home page passes the validation tests, figure 11.9 appears.

You can now add the HTML checked image to your home page if you want. The WebTechs Validation Service even gives you the HTML you need to add to your home page. All you have to do is highlight the text and choose Edit, Copy from the menu bar. Then, pick a good place in your HTML document (probably toward the end of the page) and choose Edit, Paste to paste it into your home page in HotDog.

Icon for your home page

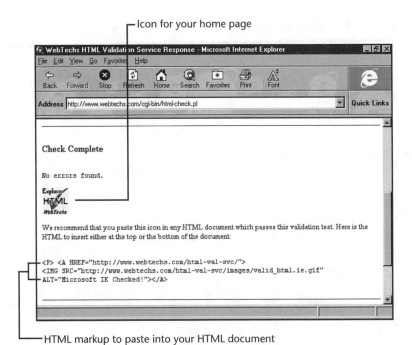

Fig. 11.9
Hooray, my home page is valid!

HTML markup to paste into your HTML document

Issues for AOL Web Authors

Once you know you have good, valid HTML documents ready for the Web, it's time to upload them to My Place. This is just about the last place you can introduce problems for your Web site—but this doesn't make these problems uncommon.

We discussed the uploading process all the way back in Chapter 2, but I do need to remind you of a couple of things that can go wrong during the upload. Especially as your site gets more complicated, you'll have to pay particular care to the following couple of issues:

■ **Make sure you don't have any local file references**—HotDog does a bad thing, and we talked about it in Chapter 7. Sometimes, when creating a link, HotDog will try to add the link with an URL like **file:// /C|web_site/about.htm**. That URL will not work once the file is uploaded to My Place, since it's designed to point to a file on your hard drive. If you're going to store all of your Web files in the My Place directory (as opposed to in separate subdirectories), your links just need to be in the form SRC="image.gif" or HREF="about.htm".

- **Name your files correctly**—This is especially important when uploading to the My Place directory. If you change the name of any of your files—like your graphics files or other pages for your site—you'll break the links to those files on your home page. If you name a file me.gif when you upload it to My Place, but you've created an <IMG SRC> link on your home page to self.gif, that picture link will be broken when your user tries to load your home page.

- **Give your files the correct filename extension**—Here's another fun problem. You need to use the correct filename extensions when uploading to My Place, for two reasons. First, many browsers need to see a valid file extension when downloading multimedia files. So, make sure your graphics and multimedia clips end with standard filename extensions. Also remember that the extension is important for URLs. If you use a different extension when uploading to My Place, you'll break links to that document or file on your home page.

> **Caution**
>
> One of the most common problems people have when uploading to My Place is forgetting which HTML file extension convention (.htm versus .html) they used. If you've used .htm through your pages, you need to stick to it when you upload your files to My Place. Otherwise, none of your links will work.

- **Test everything after uploading**—You should always test your site once it's actually on the Web, just to make sure that you're happy with what the entire world will see from you. Take special care, though, to check the special AOL-specific elements, like the AOL Web counter, if you've decided to use it. Also, don't forget to click all your links and try downloading any multimedia files you've added—just to make sure they all work perfectly.

CHAPTER 12

Publicizing Your Web Page

Once your home page is finished and available on the Web, hordes and hordes of people will stop by for a look because they want to see it, right? Not if nobody knows about your page. Without publicity and home page advertisements, no one will even know that you have a home page, let alone stop by.

That's where this chapter comes into play. In it, you'll learn how to announce to the Internet and WWW world that your page is up and ready for visitors. I'll teach you how to create and place home page advertisements in hot spots around the Internet.

Promoting Your Web Presence

Have you seen the movie *Field of Dreams*? Unfortunately, the "if you build it, they will come" philosophy doesn't work as well on the WWW as it does with baseball ghosts. You've got to do some legwork and spread the word about your home page if you want to attract traffic.

Businesses understand this philosophy, and so should you. When a company creates a brand new product, they generally have to spend thousands (if not millions) of dollars advertising it in magazines and newspapers, and on the television and radio. Fortunately, publicizing your home page is free; your only cost is the time you spend telling other WWW surfers about it. But this time is well spent.

Before you start advertising your home page on the WWW, you should first think through why you are publicizing your home page, who you are announcing it to, and what kind of results to expect. By thinking this through, you'll have a better idea of what your overall goal is behind announcing to the WWW that you have a home page.

> **Note**
>
> Before you can publicize your home page, you've got to upload it onto the Internet. See "Where to Put Your Web Pages" in Chapter 2 for more information about finding the right spot on AOL for uploading your home page.

Why Publicize Your Web Page?

For your home page, you're probably advertising for personal satisfaction. If you installed a counter (see Chapter 8), you want to see how many people stop by your home page—it's almost like a contest. Another reason might be because your home page revolves around a particular hobby. You want to publicize your page so other like-minded individuals will stop by.

Business home pages usually have ulterior motives. They might advertise their products or services, or simply try to impress visitors. The Coca-Cola home page that I mentioned in Chapter 2 is a prime example of this. You're not going to buy soft drinks through the Internet, but just having a WWW presence is good publicity.

Of course, many people don't even care about advertising their home page. They use their home page as a personal starting point on the WWW, and customize it for their use only. They create lists of links that interest them, and spots they like to visit. Their home page is more like a home base, where they just check in every now and then. If this is you, why spend lots of time publicizing your home page if you don't care who visits it?

> **Tip**
>
> Want to use your home page as the default page in IE? Start by loading your page. Then, choose View, Options. In the Options dialog box, click the Start and Search Pages tab, and then click the button Use Current. Now whatever page you have loaded will be your starting point.

Set Reasonable Expectations

Most likely, advertising your home page will increase the number of visitors you get. Originally, my home page was getting about five visits a day, ranging from my friends to random visitors. Once I started to publicize my home page all over the Internet, my daily tally started increasing rapidly. Eventually, I was averaging around 100 visitors a day. Of course I have no idea whether they liked my home page, found it useful, or ever came back.

After awhile, the daily visitor count started to taper off to about 10–15 visits a day. Don't expect basic advertising techniques to attract millions of visitors— set reasonable expectations so you're not disappointed.

> **Note**
>
> While you may be lucky to get a couple of hundred people to visit your home page, some sites get thousands of visitors a day. That's because they offer a unique service that piques the curiosity of many people, and keeps them coming back again and again. For example, Mirksy's Worst of the Web (**http://mirsky.com/wow/**) gets thousands of people daily because it is a creative and constantly updated site. See "Keep Your Home Page Alive" in Chapter 11 for more information on maintaining interest on your home page.

Publicizing on AOL

Since you more than likely deal with the AOL service relatively frequently, it's an excellent place to start publicizing your page. One quick trick is to simply make your Web URL part of your signature when you send e-mail messages or respond in message groups. You don't want to get too carried away with advertisements in messages, but a simple two line tag can't hurt too much (see fig. 12.1).

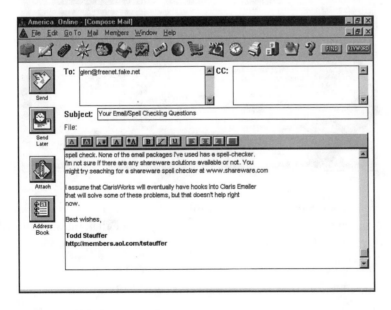

Fig. 12.1
This is the simplest way to get your URL out to the AOL public.

This has the distinct advantage of playing to a captive, controlled demo-graphic—something many corporate advertisers love to find. Basically, you're just letting your friends, colleagues, and online acquaintances get easy access to your home page. It's especially helpful if you spend a lot of time in the same message areas that reflect the interests on your Web page.

Even if you spend a lot of time in the People Connection online "chat" groups, you'll want to let folks know your Web address. In fact, that might be all the publicity you need, or care, to do.

Publicizing through the Web Diner

If you're ready to take the next step online, head over to the Web Cafe (key-word **Web Diner**) where the Web designers on AOL tend to hang out. Not only can you get some advice and discussion time for your Web design here, but it's a great place to drum up some publicity. Where? Start with the Family Recipes section in the Web Diner's menu (see fig. 12.2).

Fig. 12.2
A simple e-mail and you're included in the Web Diner home page listing.

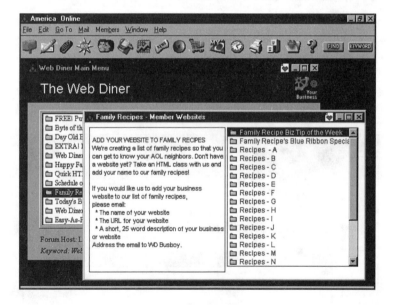

Once you've got your page up and running, all you need to do is send an e-mail message to the screen name **WDBusboy**. The e-mail message should include the following:

- The name of your Web site (e.g., Billy's World)
- The URL (e.g., **http://members.aol.com/billyq/**)
- A short, approximately 25-word description of your page

And that's it! Fire off that e-mail message and you'll be placed in the Web Diner listing.

Other Web Diner Publicity

In the next section, we'll start discussing some of the sites for publicizing on the entire Web—instead of just on AOL. But, before we do, I just wanted you to know that you can get to some of these sites (and a few we won't discuss) from the Web Diner main menu. It's just a convenient way to see them all in one listing.

From the Web Diner main menu, you should see an option that says "FREE! Put Up Your Web Site." If you do, double-click that. You'll be offered another menu, where you'll find a menu item to Publicize Your Web Site. Now double-click that option and you're presented with something that should look like figure 12.3.

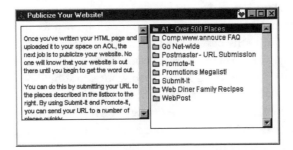

Fig. 12.3
It's easy to get at many of the publicity Web sites we'll discuss in a moment, right from the Web Diner.

> **Note**
>
> Of course, AOL moves things around every once in a while, but this is a valuable resource. If it's not exactly where I said it was, look around in the Web Diner and at keyword **HTML**.

Using WWW Catalogs and Announcement Services

The easiest and most popular way to advertise your home page is by using existing WWW catalogs, announcement services, and indexes. These places are there specifically to publicize new and popular WWW sites all over the world.

Announcement services are like a town crier standing on the corner. They constantly list loads of new home pages for all of the Web public to read and see. Every type of home page imaginable is listed in these public pages.

Related to announcement services, WWW catalogs create searchable lists of Web pages that they know about. You can search a WWW catalog for a specific topic or key word. Finally, WWW indexes actually go out on their own and search the WWW for new pages. They add every page they find to a huge database and let WWW surfers search for different Web sites.

Announcement Services

Announcement services such as the Netscape What's New pages are publicly available sites that anyone can use to announce their home page. You submit a blurb about your home page, and your information will soon appear on their What's New pages for thousands of WWW surfers to see.

These services receive thousands of submissions weekly. Typically, any type of Web page is accepted and listed in these announcement services. They're a great place to start your home page publicity.

GNN Select's New Sites

GNN, the Internet arm of AOL, is becoming well-known for its attempts to catalog and organize the best of the Web. One of the services, GNN Select (**http://www.gnn.com/gnn/wic/wics/index.html**) offers a special area for New Sites to the Web. To be listed, your site should be rather unique and able to hold the interest of a fairly broad audience. Head over to the GNN Select New Sites listing (**http://www.gnn.com/gnn/wic/wics/nunu.new.html**) to see what the competition looks like and gauge your site's chances of making the list (see fig. 12.4.)

Fig. 12.4
GNN Select organizes and updates its listing of new sites as they appear on the Web.

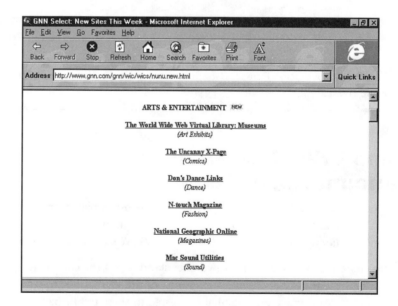

If you submit your URL to the WebCrawler search engine, then it's automatically submitted to the GNN Select service. If you haven't yet dealt with WebCrawler, you can enter your URL for GNN Select directly. Just head over to the GNN Select Submission page at **http://www.gnn.com/gnn/wic/wics/support/submission.html** and enter your URL (see fig. 12.5).

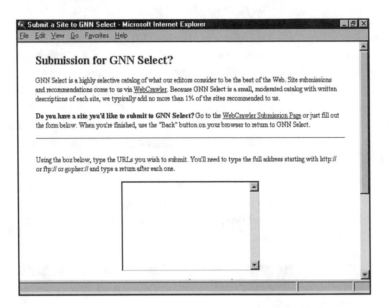

Fig. 12.5
Enter your URL on the submissions page to be considered for GNN Select.

The GNN Select service claims it only accepts about one percent of submissions for the catalog. If you make it, rest assured that you're in good Web company!

> **Note**
>
> If you happen to be using a browser that doesn't support forms, you can also submit your URL to WebCrawler/GNN by sending e-mail to **wc@webcrawler.com**.

WWW Directories

Unlike announcement services, WWW directories are catalogs of thousands of Web pages. Some, like Yahoo, are organized by category; others are huge listings of home pages. You can stop by these directories and browse or search for a specific entry.

WWW directories are great places to advertise your home page because once your entry is accepted, it will always be listed in the pertinent category. For example, if your home page centers around baseball, you can add it to the Yahoo catalog. Then anyone who searches through the catalog looking for baseball will find your home page. You don't have to rely on their reading and announcement page on the right day to see your home page.

Yahoo

Yahoo (**http://www.yahoo.com**) is the biggest, oldest, and most-used WWW index. Started a couple of years ago by two Stanford University students, Yahoo has grown to become the best spot to find Web sites on nearly every page imaginable. Yahoo is my personal favorite WWW directory, and I use it almost every day. With over 50,000 entries, if a subject isn't listed in the Yahoo directory, you'll likely have trouble finding it elsewhere on the Web.

Anyone can submit entries for their home (or business) pages (see fig. 12.6). You get to choose from the available list of Yahoo categories and then type important information describing your site. To add new entries, go to **http://www.yahoo.com/bin/add**.

Fig. 12.6
Once you're listed in Yahoo, you should get a consistent stream of visitors to your home page.

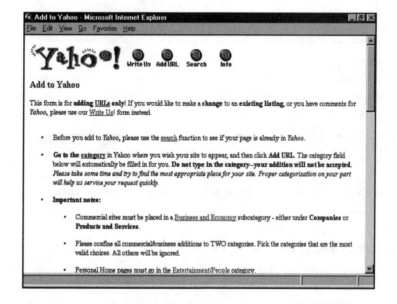

> **Note**
>
> The folks at Yahoo actually suggest that you go to the category that you think is appropriate for your Web site, and then click the Add URL button once you're there. That helps them organize things better. All business sites should be in Business and Commerce and personal sites should be listed under Entertainment:People.

Official World Wide Web Yellow Pages

Claiming status as the official World Wide Web Yellow Pages, this site is sponsored by New Riders Press (a sister imprint to Que) (**http://www.mcp.com/nrp/wwwyp/**). You can buy an actual copy of the Official World Wide Web Yellow Pages and flip through the organized listings of WWW sites, or search through this online index (whichever is your preference). Remember that the online index is constantly updated and will likely contain up-to-date information. To add new entries, go to **http://www.mcp.com/nrp/wwwyp/submit.html**.

Shown in figure 12.7, this site resembles your friendly phone book. Users can search for Web pages by a key word or category, and even add their own home page to the list. I recommend including your home page in this directory because of its ever-increasing popularity (and on the next printing, it will even appear in the book!).

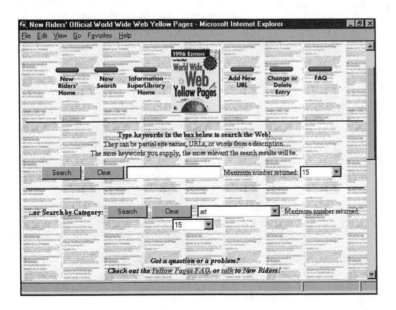

Fig. 12.7
A cyberspace phone book, the WWW Yellow Pages is one of the best directories on the Web.

Searching the WWW

Similar to WWW directories, there are several available WWW search tools which will reach out and search thousands of different WWW sites for information. Nicknamed WWW *spiders*, many of these search tools crawl from WWW page to WWW page looking for queried information. They use the links found on one page to bring them to new and different links, thus traveling the WWW like a spider.

I've listed two popular WWW search tools here. You can add your page to these tools and let their WWW spiders creep into your home page!

Lycos

The first five letters of the Latin word for wolf spider, Lycos (**http://www.lycos.com/**) boasts that it is the catalog of the WWW. Indexing millions of WWW documents, Lycos is constantly traveling the WWW looking for new pages to add to its index (see fig. 12.8). Users can submit a search query and Lycos will return WWW pages according to how well they matched your query. To submit new entries, go to **http://www.lycos.com/register.html**.

Fig. 12.8
Lycos never gets tired. It explores the Web all day and night.

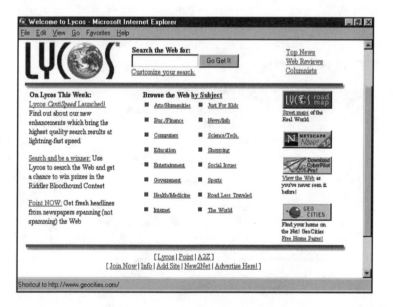

Lycos actively encourages anyone who creates a WWW page to add it to their index. They want to have the most comprehensive index available. In fact, Lycos may already have your home page listed. Since their spider is constantly crawling through the Web, it adds new Web pages as they are found, whether or not you request to be in their index.

Tip

If for some reason you do not want to be included in the Lycos catalog, but the spider has already found you, choose Delete Your Own Pages from the Lycos register page.

Note

Don't worry if your home page doesn't immediately appear in the searchable in-dex—give it some time to crawl over to your Web page. (In fact, they're currently asking for you to have at least six weeks' worth of patience.)

WebCrawler

Owned and run by America Online, WebCrawler is another popular WWW Search Service (**http://Webcrawler.com/**) (see fig. 12.9). It fields nearly 250,000 searches every month and has visited hundreds of thousands of WWW pages.

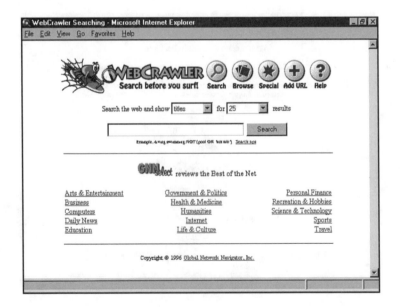

Fig. 12.9
Although WebCrawler is smaller than Lycos, it's used extremely often, especially by AOL members.

You can add your home page to WebCrawler's list of URLs to visit, explore, and index. To add new entries, go to **http://Webcrawler.com/WebCrawler/SubmitURLS.html**.

> **Tip**
>
> WebCrawler has a URL pointer that lets visitors go to any page included in its index at random. Similar to a roulette wheel, WebCrawler lets WWW surfers explore new Web sites (maybe even yours) that they have never visited. Click Random Links to explore this WWW game of roulette.

Submit It!—17 WWW Catalogs in One

The fastest and easiest way to publicize your home page on the WWW might just be Submit It! (**http://www.submit-it.com/**). This one-stop publicity site lets you fill out one form and submit your home page to 17 of the most popular indexes and catalogs of WWW pages (including Yahoo, Lycos, WebCrawler, and the official WWW Yellow Pages).

Here's how it works. You fill out an entry at the Submit It! site. Automatically, your home page information will be sent to all of the WWW indexes and catalogs shown in figure 12.10. Each site then reads your request and decides whether or not to add your entry.

Fig. 12.10

Submit It! lets you add your home page to many WWW catalogs in one shot.

Unfortunately, using Submit It! has several drawbacks. You only get to choose your category once. Each of the catalogs has a slightly different set of categories, so you never get to choose a perfectly optimized category for any of them (which is extremely important for catalogs such as Yahoo).

Additionally, no records are kept to let you know where you have submitted your home page. Also, you might not know whether or not your submission has been accepted. You have to check most of them out individually to see if your home page made it. Still, Submit It! is a great place for you to get a lot of publicizing done quickly.

Using UseNet Newsgroups

Besides the WWW, newsgroups are one of the most popular applications available on the Internet. Organized into many different categories, newsgroups let people from all over the world hold virtual conversations. I could post a question from my home in Colorado Springs, CO, and receive responses from California, Mexico, and Australia.

There are literally thousands of different newsgroups, ranging in interest from Microsoft Windows to automobiles—and covering everything in between. Posting messages to newsgroups is a great way to publicize your home page because it's cheap and reaches a large audience.

comp.infosystems.www.announce

The sole purpose for this newsgroup is to announce new Web pages and HTML services and tools. This is a very high-traffic newsgroup (several hundred posts a week). It is a moderated newsgroup (meaning someone reads every message before it is posted throughout the world), and messages must follow a strict format, or else they'll be rejected.

You can post to **comp.infosystems.www.announce** directly through Netscape. Go to **news:comp.infosystems.www.announce**.

Then click the Post a Message button at the top of the screen to bring up the Send Mail/Post News dialog box. Type in the message subject and body. Your message's subject should contain one of the following listed words in all caps, followed by an accurate description of what can be found there:

ARCHIVE	ENTERTAINMENT	MAGAZINE	SCIENCE
ART	ENVIRONMENT	MISC	SERVER
BOOK	FAQ	MUSIC	SHOPPING
BROWSER	GAMES	NEWS	SOFTWARE
COLLECTION	HEALTH	PERSONAL	SPORTS
ECONOMY	HUMANITIES	POLITICS	TRANSPORTATION
EDUCATION	INFO	REFERENCE	
EMPLOYMENT	LAW	RELIGION	

If the message's subject is not correct and accurate, the newsgroup posting may be rejected. Here are some examples of good message subjects:

- PERSONAL: Todd Stauffer's home page about movies and writing books
- SPORTS: The Unofficial Texas Rangers Baseball Page
- BOOK: Creating Your Own AOL Web Pages

Likewise, here are some bad message subjects (these certainly might cause messages to be rejected):

- PERSONAL: My home page
- A simple Web page for my alma mater
- Software: Playing games

In your message body, it's important to include the full URL to the page you are announcing. Also, limit the message body to 75 lines (no one will read a message that long anyway). When you're ready, click the Send button. Your posting will appear within 48 hours.

Tip

If you have trouble posting to newsgroups, you can also submit announcements via Internet mail. Include all of the same information in the subject and body and address the message to **www-announce@boutell.com**.

Personal Newsgroup Interests

Comp.infosystems.www.announce is only the first newsgroup where you'll want to post an announcement message. Most likely, several other newsgroups will also be interested in knowing about your home page.

Search through your available newsgroups to find others that are related to your home page. If your page has a lot of information about musical theatre, for instance, you might want to post an announcement to **rec.arts.theatre.musicals** or **alt.stagecraft** to attract like-minded individuals.

Don't forget to check out newsgroups that are local to your city, state, or information provider. The University of Colorado, Colorado, and Colorado Springs all have their own local newsgroups, and since that's where I live, it would be appropriate for me to post a message in them.

Caution

Make sure you don't go overboard in advertising your home page to lots of different newsgroups. If it comes up in the discussion, feel free to point out your Web site. But posting a message about your home page to every single newsgroup you can find, regardless of its subject, is considered bad etiquette. You'll likely be reprimanded by newsgroup participants. (You may be better off including something in your UseNet signature that offers your site's URL.)

Other Ways to Advertise Your Home Page

Using WWW catalogs and Internet newsgroups are not the only ways to publicize your home page. These ways may attract a lot of initial attention, but to keep visitors coming to your home page you've got to continually plug it wherever you can (and when it is acceptable).

Resumes and Business Cards

I include my home page's URL on my resume and business cards. Since I'm proud of the work that I've done, I invite clients and prospective business associates to stop by for a visit.

Since home pages are so flexible, I can arrange mine however I like. When people stop by, it gives them a chance to learn a lot more about my interests and even lets them send e-mail to me directly.

Signing Your Mail and News Postings

Another popular way of getting the word out is including information in every e-mail message and newsgroup posting you make. At the bottom of every message I send out, I include my name and the URL of my home page like this:

> **Todd A. Stauffer**
> **tstauffer@aol.com**
> **<http://members.aol.com/tstauffer/>**

This lets anyone who reads my message know that I have a home page and where to find it should they want to visit.

Ask Other WWW Sites to Link to You

Another way to attract visitors is by asking people who maintain other pages on similar topics to include a link to your page. If my main interest is flying, for example, I could e-mail the Webmasters at local flying clubs or particular airports and ask them to link to my page—perhaps in exchange for me linking to their pages.

Send e-mail to other Web page creators out there who have pages related to yours. Tell them about your home page and give them your URL. Ask them (nicely) to include a link to your page and tell them you will reciprocate. Most likely, they'll be as excited as you are about linking their pages to a new site.

Send Your URL to Me

Finally, you can relax, sit back, and wait for the users to start hitting your site. Just watch that hit counter roll over. If you're still not getting much response, maybe you need to improve the content, expand your pages, find a cooler hobby, or get yourself on local TV morning chat shows.

But, before you settle in, there's one other bit of publicity you can do. Send the URL to me in an e-mail message. In exchange for linking your page to mine (**http://members.aol.com/tstauffer**, just in case you forgot), I'll put you on a special page of Creating AOL Pages readers' sites. Just send an e-mail message with **Creating URL** in the subject heading. If you'd like, you can tell me a little about the page in the body of the message (or say anything else). If I get enough response, I'll categorize the pages appropriately.

Congratulations on your Web presence. You've graduated to an official Web creator. (The decoder ring is in the mail.) Now, take this knowledge with you, go forth, and update your site! ❖

Appendixes

APPENDIX A

AOL Online Web Resources

Listed in this appendix are some of the places to visit on the AOL service (and sites associated with AOL, but found on the Web) to help you as you create your Web pages. When applicable, I've included the America Online keyword command for going directly to the area, if it's on the AOL service. To reach any area using a keyword, use the Ctrl+K (⌘+K on the Mac) keyboard combination for the Keyword dialog box in the AOL client software.

AOL Service Areas

A number of areas on the service are designed specifically to help you create Web pages using AOL's free Web server space for members.

Web Page Toolkit

Keyword: **HTML**

For a quick online overview of AOL's services, help groups, chat areas, and download sites, check out the Web Page toolkit. Most of this area consists of links to other areas that are discussed in this appendix, including Personal Publisher, My Place, and the Web Diner.

This is a great place to start, though, with links to different parts of the service that relate to HTML. Included are Web message board links; HTML tips, pointers, style guides; and a download library of publishing tools.

Personal Publisher

Keyword: **Personal Publisher**

This area is for creating an AOL Home Page, using tools built into the system itself. While it doesn't allow for as much freedom as the My Place Web service does, it makes getting a page up on the Web quick and easy. Included at the Personal Publisher main page are links to other resources, including a Web tutorial, archives of graphics for your Web site, and information about the PicturePlace and PictureWeb services.

Note that Personal Publisher URLs differ slightly from the My Place URLs, following the format **http://home.aol.com/***screenname*.

PicturePlace

Keyword: **PicturePlace**

Send in your traditional still photos and PicturePlace (also PictureWeb) will scan them into electronic files and place them on the Web for you to download. (If you request it, it'll also put them in your Home Page directory if you use the Personal Publisher service.) At the time of writing, it offers two free scans to interested Web authors on AOL.

My Place

Keyword: **My Place**

Here's where the FTP interface is available for all AOL members to upload their Web pages, graphics, and multimedia files for inclusion on their personal Web site. Clicking the Go to My Place button brings up a standard AOL FTP interface, complete with tools for uploading, deleting, and renaming files and adding subdirectories.

Note that My Place URLs follow the format **http://members.aol.com/** *screenname*.

Since each AOL account can actually have up to five screen names, a single account actually has up to 10 MB of storage available for its Web site. The site needs to be divided into (up to) five separate chunks of 2 MB each, which need to be spread among the five different URLs.

Web Diner

Keyword: **Web Diner**

Web Diner is one of the major resources for AOL-based Web authors. Here you can find tidbits, discussion groups, help, links to other relevant areas on AOL, hyperlinks to useful Web areas, and much more. The service, sponsored in part by a Web-based design firm (**http://www.webdiner.com/**), features a live chat area, a fairly active message area, and software archives. It's a great place to try the latest HTML editing programs, find useful templates, or learn more about creating HTML pages for the AOL service.

It's also the heart of AOL's links to the home pages of other members and to the various publicity tools that you can use to make your site more visible to the outside world. You can even take an HTML class through the Web Diner main menu!

AOL Web Sites

http://members.aol.com/

Using the AOL Web browser, you can get to this home base for the My Place service on AOL. Here's where anyone on the Web can search for your home page, browse through all of the home pages made available through AOL, or just learn more about the service.

http://home.aol.com/

Although similar to the members page above, this one concentrates on helping Web users find AOL members who've elected to use the Personal Publisher home page service.

http://www.aol.com/

This main page for AOL on the Web is a mixed bag of useful resources, including information about the AOL service and the company, recent developments in AOL's offers, and links to other useful and interesting sites. Although it doesn't relate tons of information on HTML or AOL's Web services, it is a useful jumping off point for folks interested in learning more about AOL or the Web. ❖

Appendixes

Home Page Final Checklist

Listed in this appendix is a final checklist you should use when you've just about finished creating your home page. Before you make it publicly available, run through this simple checklist to make sure you've caught most of the common mistakes new home page creators make. Here, I've summarized some of the common tips and tricks that I talked about throughout the book.

Basic HTML

- The important \<HTML\> \</HTML\>, \<HEAD\> \</HEAD\>, and \<BODY\> \</BODY\> tags are included on my home page.
- Home page is properly titled using the \<TITLE\> and \</TITLE\> tags.
- HTML tags have their respective closing tags (i.e., \<H1\> and \</H1\>).
- Home page shows name and e-mail address and the date that the page was last changed, using the \<ADDRESS\> tags.
- The \<P\> tag is used to separate paragraphs of text (instead of nothing or the \<BR\> tag).

Lists and Tables

- Replaced large paragraphs with lists and tables wherever possible.
- Used the Tab key to line up lists and each list item in the HTML source file for internal documentation purposes.
- All the rows in the HTML table have the same number of columns and vice versa.
- Used row and column headers in my tables.

Links

- Didn't overuse WWW links on my home page by linking virtually every word.
- Made important words and phrases hot so visitors know where they're linking.
- Links have been recently tested and work properly.
- Links to large images and audio and video files are labeled with the size of the file they download.
- Internal targets use descriptive names within the page and the links to them work correctly.

Images

- All home page images are around 20K or less in file size.
- Entire home page, images and all, is smaller than 100K.
- Images larger than 20K have smaller, thumbnail size images on home page that link visitors to the larger images (and those thumbnails were actually created in a graphics program, not with the HEIGHT and WIDTH attributes).
- The full path and filename to each image is correct.
- Background pattern isn't too busy and confusing.
- Text placed on top of my background pattern is easily read, and the background color and text color are not too similar.
- Images properly align with the text next to them.

Other

- Checked page in Internet Explorer and other browsers (if possible) before making it available online.
- There are no misspelled words on the page.
- Used HTML comments for internal documentation purposes.
- HTML source file is readable and easy to update.
- Placed an exact backup of the page and all associated files (images, audio, etc.) in a safe place—just in case.

Uploading to My Place

- Copied exact names of all files to be uploaded on a sheet of paper.

- Signed onto AOL using appropriate screen name.

- Uploaded files using same, exact filename (include the same file extensions) that I used when creating the site.

- Tested site in Internet Explorer (including appearance, all links, and all graphics).

- Checked AOL odometer-style counter on the page (if applicable) to make sure it's begun counting.

- Tested site in old AOL browser (if possible) or another browser to test appearance in non-Netscape compatible (or HTML 3.2 compatible) browsers.

- Checked to make sure URL to home page is working correctly (**http://members.aol.com/***screenname***).

References Used in This Book

This appendix consists of the links that I've talked about and used through-out this book, including examples and references. I've organized them by category so you can easily scan through this list for links useful to you.

Useful Home Page Links

HTML 2.0 Definition

http://www.w3.org/hypertext/WWW/MarkUp/html-spec/html-pubtext.html

HTML 3.2 Announcement

http://www.w3.org/pub/WWW/MarkUp/Wilbur/

The Hotdog Home Page

http://www.sausage.com

WWW Browsers

Internet Explorer

http://microsoft.com/ie/

Netscape Navigator

http://www.netscape.com/

Mosaic—another popular graphical browser

http://www.ncsa.uiuc.edu/SDG/Software/SDGSoftDir.html

Lynx—text-only browser

http://www.cc.ukans.edu/about_lynx/about_lynx.html

Arena—UNIX-based HTML 3.x test browser

http://www.w3.org/hypertext/WWW/Arena/

HTML Validation Tools

WebTechs HTML Validation Service

http://www.webtechs.com/html-val-svc/

Weblint—the HTML style and syntax checker

http://www.khoros.unm.edu/staff/neilb/weblint.html

MOMSpider—automatically checks links

http://www.ics.uci.edu/WebSoft/MOMspider/

Checker—also checks links automatically

**http://www.ugrad.cs.ubc.ca/spider/q7f192/branch/
win-checker.html**

Home Page Counters

Web Counter—the simple, non-AOL counter

http://www.digits.com/

Cool WWW Pages

The Net Movie Site

http://www.spe.sony.com/Pictures/SonyMovies/netmulti.html

Microsoft's Technical Support Page

http://www.microsoft.com/Support/

Land's End Online Catalog

http://www.landsend.com/

clnet online

http://www.cnet.com/

ESPN SportsZone

http://espnet.sportszone.com/

Coca-Cola Company

http://www.cocacola.com/

The Weather Channel's Home Page

http://www.weather.com/

Mirksy's Worst of the Web

http://mirsky.com/wow/

An interactive tour through the Louvre

http://watt.emf.net/wm/

The NASA Shuttle Site

http://shuttle.nasa.gov/

CNN Video Vault

http://www.cnn.com/video_vault/index.html

Books Stacks Unlimited

http://www.books.com/

Que's Home Page

http://www.mcp.com/que/

Apple Computer

http://www.apple.com/

Star Trek Voyager Home Page

http://voyager.paramount.com/VoyagerActive.html

Todd Stauffer's Home Page

http://members.aol.com/tstauffer

Andy Shafran's Home Page

http://www.shafran.com/

Site where this book's technical editor is Webmaster

http://www.union.uiuc.edu/

Roxanne's Home Page

http://www.geocities.com/CapitolHill/1099/

Appendixes

Yahoo's Flying Clubs

http://www.yahoo.com/Recreation/Aviation/Clubs/

Multimedia Clips and Information

Audio Clip Sites:

- **http://sunsite.unc.edu/pub/multimedia/sun-sounds/movies/**
- **http://www.tvtrecords.com/toons.html/**
- **http://web.msu.edu/vincent/index.html**
- **http://www.acm.uiuc.edu/rml/**

Audio File Format FAQ:

- **http://www.cis.ohio-state.edu/hypertext/faq/usenet/ audio-fmts/top.html**

Video Clip Sites:

- **http://w3.eeb.ele.tue.nl/mpeg/index.html**
- **http://www.acm.uiuc.edu/rml/**
- **http://deathstar.rutgers.edu/people/bochkay/movies.html**

MPEG Specifications:

- **http://www.cis.ohio-state.edu/hypertext/faq/usenet/ mpeg-faq/top.html**

QT Technical Specifications:

- **http://www.cast.uni-linz.ac.at/st/staff/rm/QTquickcam/**

AVI Technical Information:

- **http://www.microsoft.com**

PictureWeb—Scanning Home Photos for Web Pages:

- **http://www.pictureweb.com/**

Publicity Links

Yahoo Directory

http://www.yahoo.com

Official Web Yellow Pages

http://www.mcp.com/nrp/wwwyp/

Lycos WWW Page

http://www.lycos.com/

WebCrawler WWW Index

http://webcrawler.com/

Submit It! Publicity Page

http://www.submit-it.com/

WWW Announcements newsgroup

news:comp.infosystems.www.announce

Web Diner—company that host's AOL's Web Diner area

http://www.webdiner.com/

Places on AOL

Internet Services

keyword: **Internet**

HTML Resources on AOL

keyword: **HTML**

Personal Publisher area—basic home page creation

keyword: **Personal Publisher**

Web Diner—tips, tools, and help for Web pages

keyword: **Web Diner**

My Place—FTP uploads for your home page files

keyword: **My Place** ❖

What's on the CD-ROM?

You need three things when you build your own Web page—Web page building materials, tools, and creativity. The *Creating Your Own AOL Web Pages* CD-ROM provides you with an extensive collection of materials and tools for building your own Web page. However, you must supply the creativity. We've also included a lot of other useful goodies such as viewers and compression programs in the CD-ROM. All of the materials and programs are easy to browse through and download right through your Web browser.

Browse the CD

Browse the *Creating Your Own AOL Web Pages* CD-ROM through Web pages. You can easily access everything on the CD by firing up your Web browser and loading APPCD.HTM from the CD. For instance, if your CD-ROM drive is drive D, then the URL is **file:d:\appcd.htm**. Or, in Internet Explorer, choose File, Open to bring up the Open dialog box. Click the Browse button to begin searching for the file. Select your CD-ROM drive, click APPCD, and click the Open button.

Mostly, you'll find the following four types of links on each Web page:

- Links to other pages
- Links to materials or applications
- Links to folders on the CD (see fig. D.1)
- Links to resources on the Internet

Fig. D.1

This is a listing of the files in the BUTTONS folder on the CD-ROM.

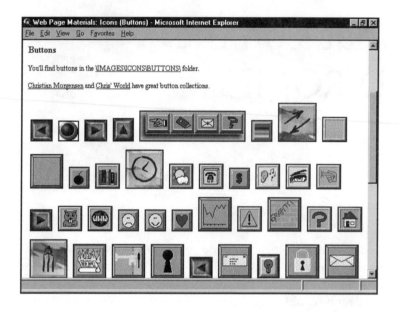

On the Buttons page, you can see the link to the BUTTONS folder filled with button files on the CD-ROM. The mouse cursor (pointing hand) is pointing to the BUTTONS folder. Below the BUTTONS folder are two links to Web pages on the Internet—Christian Morgensen's Home Page and Chris World.

When you click a link to a folder, either the folder's contents are loaded into the browser, as shown in figure D.2, or a separate folder window is opened up (depending on the browser that you use). In either case, you can easily view any file in the folder by double-clicking it, or you can copy the file to your hard drive using the usual method for your particular browser. (In Netscape, hold down your Shift button and click the file. The Save As dialog box will open. Then, follow the usual procedures. If you're using Internet Explorer, drag-and-drop the files to the Windows desktop or to a folder on your hard drive.)

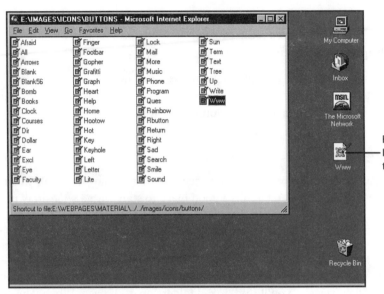

Fig. D.2
Viewing a directory of files (on the CD) in Internet Explorer.

File dragged from Internet Explorer to the desktop

Installing and Saving Files onto Your Computer

Install programs onto your computer by clicking the link associated with To Install [This Program] Click Here, under Installation Instructions.

Note

If you're using Netscape, the Save As dialog box will appear. Netscape doesn't offer a good way to launch individual programs through links. However, you can fool it into doing a pretty good job. Here's how:

1. Choose Options, General Preferences to open the Preferences dialog box.

2. Click the Helpers tab.

3. Scroll down and highlight Application/Octet-Stream in the file type list.

4. Click the Launch the Application radio button. It's one of the Action radio buttons toward the bottom of the Preferences dialog box.

5. Click OK.

Now when you click a link to a setup program, the Save As dialog box appears. Click the Cancel button and you should see a setup program launch. Follow the setup program's instructions.

Appendixes

If you're using Internet Explorer, you don't need to do any of the previous steps. When you click a setup program link, the program's installation screen will appear almost immediately.

Sometimes you need to copy program files to your computer. If you're using Windows 95 with Netscape or Internet Explorer, generally all you need to do is right-click a link to get the option to save it to disk.

Web Page Materials

Like any building project, you must begin with good raw materials to build a good Web page. This section is a good place to start with a wide array of icons, background images, templates, and links to sites on the Web.

Much of the building materials on the CD are linked to pages that you can browse with your Web browser. All that you need to do is point and click what you want to get at. However, there's simply too much material to link it all to Web pages so you'll find linked folders on each page. When you click them, they will open, showing all of the relevant material. Double-click any file that you want to examine and it'll load into your browser.

Audio

Choose from hundreds of audio files. You'll find the following general categories of sounds on the CD:

- Animal sounds
- Special effects
- Sounds from around the house
- Instrument sounds
- Sounds from nature
- Voices

Links to sound archives on the Internet are included.

> **Tip**
>
> If you're using a browser other than Internet Explorer, don't forget to set up a helper application to run WAV format sound files!

Hotlists

Use the Hotlists page to access major Web page building resources on the Internet. Most of these links will take you to huge lists of links of Internet resources useful to a Web page builder. Check out the Macmillan Winner's Circle page through the link at the bottom of the Hotlists page under Best Personal Web Page Contest. You can look at the winning Web page and enter your Web page into the contest.

Images

There are hundreds of images for you on this CD, including the following:

- Backgrounds
- Bullets
- Buttons
- Lines
- Pictures

Usually there are far too many images to include them all on the page, so be sure to check out the folders. Also, explore the links to Internet sites and lists on the Internet that'll take you to even more sites.

Templates

I have included a template for you to start you off with a working Web page (including a link to my home page). You can also open any of the Web pages included on this CD to check out how something is done or borrow pieces of code. You'll find most of the Web pages under the \WEBPAGES\ folder on the CD. Just open the files with the HTM extension using any word processor.

Video

Also included are both QuickTime and MPEG videos for you to try out. When you open the Video page, just click a linked picture. The movie will load onto your computer and run if your browser is configured to run a program that will view the video type you clicked on. Otherwise, you can either save the video file onto your hard disk or you can configure a viewer. You'll find both QuickTime and MPEG viewers on this CD. Just find the section "Viewers, Pictures, Sound, Video, and PostScript" in this appendix.

Appendixes

Tools for Building Web Pages

The right tools are essential to the builder of Web pages. We've included a large assortment of HTML editors, image map editors, and HTML converters on the CD, along with links to some useful sites on the Web.

HTML Converters

These files convert pre-existing files into the HTML format.

RTF to HTML

Use this utility to convert documents from the RTF format to HTML. RTF (Rich Text Format) is becoming the standard format used for text under Windows, especially Windows 95, where the standard word processor included with the operating system, WordPad, handles RTF. Most major word processors can import and export RTF files. This package includes a Microsoft Word 2.0 for Windows template for writing HTML.

Tex2RTF

Use this utility to convert LaTeX files to HTML. Tex2RTF also converts LaTeX to Windows Help file format if you need that capability. LaTeX is a format that's very popular for files created for print and online, and is also a common language used for technical documents. To make the most of Tex2RTF, you should read through the program's very good help system.

HTML Editors

Using HTML editors will speed up your HTML coding.

HotDog Web Editor

For a fast, flexible, and friendly way to create HTML documents, use the HotDog Web Editor. HotDog supports both Netscape extensions to HTML and HTML 3.2 elements. Its dialogs let you perform complex tasks like creating forms and tables in a few seconds. And HotDog includes many features like finding duplicate tags and converting DOS files for use on UNIX systems. You can easily set almost 50 options to set up HotDog to behave just the way you want it to.

HTML Assistant for Windows

HTML Assistant is a simple shareware HTML document editor. Most commands are implemented via a huge toolbar. The program is a good editor for small documents limited to 32K files. A unique feature of HTML Assistant is its ability to convert files that contain URLs to HTML documents that can be read with any Web browser.

HTMLed

HTMLed is a powerful shareware HTML document editor that features a toolbar and abundant and clear menus.

HTML Easy! Pro

You can easily make a Web page with HTML Easy! Pro. You can also use HTML Easy! Pro as a text editor. HTML Easy! Pro supports full HTML 3.0 commands and Netscape Extensions.

HTML HyperEdit

HTML HyperEdit is a simple editor that includes a hypermedia tutorial.

HTML Writer

HTML Writer is a stand-alone HTML authoring program. Most HTML tags can be inserted using an extensive set of menu commands. A toolbar is used to implement many HTML tags. Another feature is HTML Writer's support of templates, which you can use to help design and create HTML documents with a consistent look and feel.

Live Markup

Build or edit Web pages in the actual HTML environment directly on-screen without the necessity to learn or type any HTML tags with Live Markup. Live Markup is a WYSIWYG (What You See Is What You Get) HTML editor.

Appendixes

SoftQuad HoTMetaL

SoftQuad HoTMetaL is a full-featured, professional-quality HTML editor. With this freeware, you can edit multiple documents at the same time, use templates to ensure consistency between documents, and use its powerful word-processor-like features.

WebEdit v1.1a

WebEdit allows you to edit multiple documents at once. It has a very clean, simple interface that hides powerful features.

WebForms v1.5

Create your own forms and link them to your home page with WebForms. Responses to the forms you create are automatically sent to your mailbox, and then read by WebForms and collected in a Response Database.

HTML Editors for MS Word

If you're a Microsoft Word user, you can turn the familiar word processor into an HTML editor.

ANT_HTML

Create hypertext documents using the ANT_DEMO template for Microsoft Word 6 for Windows and Macintosh. You can insert HTML codes into any new or existing Word or ASCII document. ANT_DEMO is a demonstration version of the ANT_PLUS conversion utility and the ANT_HTML package. Both ANT_HTML and ANT_PLUS work in all international versions of Word 6.

CU_HTML

Create HTML documents in Microsoft Word 2 or 6 using the CU_HTML template.

GT_HTML

GT_HTML is a Microsoft Word 6 template for creating HTML documents. Only a small number of HTML tags are currently supported by GT_HTML, but the ones that are included are the most common tags and should be useful for many basic HTML documents.

HTML Author

HTML Author is a template for creating HTML documents in Microsoft Word 6.

Microsoft Internet Assistant for Word 6.0

Create HTML documents visually using Microsoft Internet Assistant for Word 6 for Windows. HTML tags are hidden and created automatically by the Internet Assistant. Internet Assistant also turns Word into a Web browser.

Microsoft Internet Assistant 2.0 for Word for Windows 95

Create HTML documents visually using Microsoft Internet Assistant for Word for Windows 95. HTML tags are hidden and created automatically by the Internet Assistant. Internet Assistant also turns Word into a Web browser.

WebWizard

WebWizard is an HTML authoring system that works as a template in Microsoft Word 6. A new toolbar is added to Word 6 with some HTML commands, and a new WebWizard menu is added to the menu bar.

Image Map Editors

Simplify making image maps by using an image map editor.

Mapedit

Map images using the WYSIWYG (What You See Is What You Get) image mapper Mapedit.

Map THIS!

You can map images with Map THIS!. As discussed in Chapter 9, "Clickable Image Maps and Beyond," this program is very useful for creating a map definition file, which you can then use to create server- or client-side clickable maps.

Internet-Related Applications

Materials and tools will give you most of what you need to build Web pages. Nevertheless, these additional applications come in handy when you spend a lot of time on the Web. You may want to turn your PC into a Web server or you might need a viewer for a file type that you hadn't viewed before.

Viewers, Pictures, Sound, Video, and PostScript

View any file on the Internet by having the right viewers. These programs are generally helper apps that you can configure for use with Internet Explorer or Netscape. Each has a specific purpose and can be used to view one or more multimedia file types.

GhostView v1.0

Use GhostView version 1.0 to view printer files that conform to GhostScript 2.6 or later standards. GhostScript is an interpreter for the PostScript page-description language used by many laser printers. GhostView can also be used to print GhostScript-embedded documents.

Jasc Media Center

Use Jasc Media Center to keep large collections of multimedia files organized. The program supports 37 file formats, including GIF, JPEG, MIDI, WAV, and AVI. Formats that aren't supported can still be used if you have an external file filter for them.

LView

Load, view, edit, and save image files of many different formats with LView.

Media Blastoff

View several popular graphics formats, as well as sound and movies, with Media Blastoff.

MPEGPlay

Play MPEG movies with MPEGPlay. MPEGPlay is a 32-bit program and will run under Windows 95 and Windows NT. You must use Win32s (the special Windows 3.1 32-bit extensions) to run it under 16-bit Windows.

PlayWave

Use PlayWave to play WAV sound files. PlayWave can be set to loop a wave file continuously.

QuickTime 2.0 for Windows

Play QuickTime movies (MOV) with QuickTime 2.0 for Windows. MOV files are common on the Internet.

VuePrint

Work with and view graphics in several popular formats including JPEG and GIF using VuePrint. The screen saver included with VuePrint displays image file collections. VuePrint also has a built-in UUEncoder and UUDecoder. VuePrint is an all-in-one graphics solution for most of your Internet graphics needs.

WinECJ

WinECJ is a fast JPEG viewer. The program can open multiple files and has a slide-show-presentation mode.

WPlany

WPlany plays several sound file formats found on the Internet including WAV. WPlany is an easy-to-use program.

Web Servers

Turn your PC into a Web server. If you ever feel like moving on from the AOL service and connecting your own computer to the Internet as a Web page server, you can use one of these programs (along with a high-speed connection).

Web4Ham

Web4Ham turns your PC into a Web site that other people can access with any Web-browsing software.

Windows HTTPD v1.4

Windows HTTPD has extensive online documentation in HTML format. Run only under Microsoft Windows and Windows for Workgroups 3.1 and 3.11.

Web Accessories

Here are a couple of programs to make your Web life easier.

Launcher

Launcher allows you to launch a Microsoft Windows application from a link in a Web browser. This feature allows you to open a Windows application without creating a link to a particular document.

URL Grabber Demo

If you've ever read an article in a UseNet newsgroup or an e-mail message and seen a URL that you wanted to save for further reference, then you can use URL Grabber. Sure, you can copy and paste the URL into a browser and then save it in a hotlist or bookmark, but this handy little utility makes this process even easier.

The URL Grabber toolbar enables you to grab a URL from documents as you read them and then save a collection of addresses as HTML documents that you can open in any Web browser. You then have a Web document that contains all the links to the URL addresses that you've saved, enabling you to jump to those URLs quickly and easily. (In this demo version, you are limited to grabbing three addresses each time you run the program.)

Other Applications

Don't let this other category on the CD fool you. These are probably the most used applications both on and off the Web.

Compression Software

Everyone uses compression software whether they know it or not. (Almost all software that you buy, such as Microsoft Windows, is stored as compressed files and is decompressed when installed.) File compression saves a lot of time and money by decreasing file transfer times over the Net.

ArcMaster

Use ArcMaster to compress and decompress files in many popular compression formats, including ZIP, LHZ, and ARJ. You need to have the file compression/decompression utilities for each of these. ArcMaster is a front end program that makes it easier to use the DOS utilities under Windows. It supports drag-and-drop, allows you to conveniently manipulate compressed files, and converts files from one compression format to another.

ArcShell

ArcShell is a Windows shell you can use to make it easy to manipulate ZIP, LHZ, ARC, and ARJ compression files. You need to have the file compression/decompression utilities for each of these. ArcShell acts as a front end to the DOS utilities.

Drag And Zip

Turn your Windows 3.1 File Manager into a file manager for creating and managing ZIP, LZH, and GZ files by using the Drag And Zip utilities. Drag And Zip has built-in routines to zip and unzip files that makes it very easy to compress and extract ZIP files. Drag And Zip supports copies of PKZIP, LHA, and GUNZIP to manage compressed files and has a built-in virus scanner that you can use to scan compressed files for possible viruses.

WinZip

Use WinZip 6.0 to painlessly zip and unzip files. This version has been specially developed for Windows 95. For instance, use the Add To Zip command added to Explorers context menu to quickly add files to an archive. Drag-and-drop is also supported.

Zip Manager

Zip Manager is a stand-alone Windows ZIP utility. Zip Manager doesn't require PKZIP and PKUNZIP and is 100 percent PKZIP 2.04 compatible.

Zip Master

Use Zip Master to add, freshen, or update existing ZIP files, create new ZIP files, extract from or test existing ZIP files, view existing ZIP file contents, and

many other functions. Zip Master doesn't require you to have PKZIP or
PKUNZIP.

Picture Conversion/Manipulation

Graphics is one of the things that makes the Web so intuitive and fun. So its
not surprising that a Web builder will often use picture conversion and ma-
nipulation programs. In addition to the programs here, many of the viewers
listed in the "Internet-Related Applications" section are also able to convert
and manipulate images.

Image'n'Bits

Use Image'n'Bits to manipulate and convert graphics. Among the formats
supported are BMP and GIF. Image'n'Bits is able to create special effects including dithering, pixelizing, and solarizing. If you're working with artistic
images or photographs, Image'n'Bits is very useful.

Paint Shop Pro 3

Paint Shop Pro 3 is a powerful graphics viewing and editing utility that supports about 20 different graphics file formats, including the common GIF and
JPEG formats found on the Web. Paint Shop Pro 3 has a host of features for
editing and manipulating graphics, and rivals commercial packages with its
number and variety of filters and special effects. Paint Shop Pro 3 also includes a screen-capture program.

WinJPEG

WinJPEG is a Windows-based graphics-file viewer and converter. You can
read and save TIFF, GIF, JPG, TGA, BMP, and PCX file formats with WinJPEG
and it has several color-enhancement and dithering features. WinJPEG supports batch conversions and screen captures.

WinLab

WinLab is a powerful graphics viewer and editor. In addition to WinLab's image processing features, it has built-in TWAIN and network support and a
Winsock-compliant application for sending and receiving images. ❖

Index

Check out Que® Books
on the World Wide Web
http://www.mcp.com/que

As the biggest software release in computer history, Windows 95 continues to redefine the computer industry. Click here for the latest info on our Windows 95 books

Make computing quick and easy with these products designed exclusively for new and casual users

Examine the latest releases in word processing, spreadsheets, operating systems, and suites

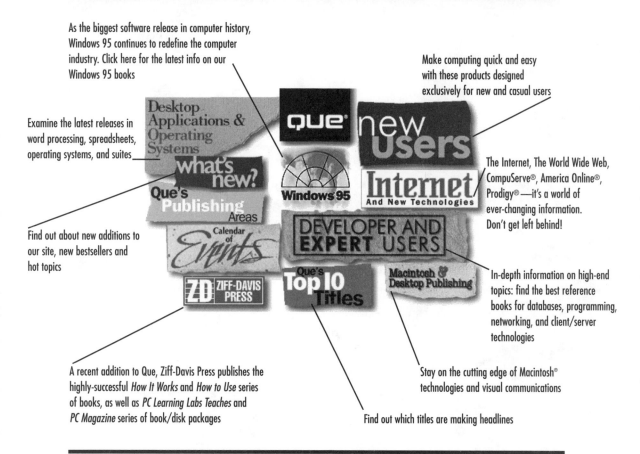

The Internet, The World Wide Web, CompuServe®, America Online®, Prodigy® —it's a world of ever-changing information. Don't get left behind!

Find out about new additions to our site, new bestsellers and hot topics

In-depth information on high-end topics: find the best reference books for databases, programming, networking, and client/server technologies

A recent addition to Que, Ziff-Davis Press publishes the highly-successful *How It Works* and *How to Use* series of books, as well as *PC Learning Labs Teaches* and *PC Magazine* series of book/disk packages

Stay on the cutting edge of Macintosh® technologies and visual communications

Find out which titles are making headlines

With 6 separate publishing groups, Que develops products for many specific market segments and areas of computer technology. Explore our Web Site and you'll find information on best-selling titles, newly published titles, upcoming products, authors, and much more.

- Stay informed on the latest industry trends and products available
- Visit our online bookstore for the latest information and editions
- Download software from Que's library of the best shareware and freeware

QUE® has the right choice for every computer user

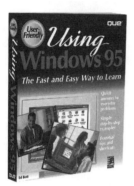

From the new computer user to the advanced programmer, we've got the right computer book for you. Our user-friendly *Using* series offers just the information you need to perform specific tasks quickly and move onto other things. And, for computer users ready to advance to new levels, QUE *Special Edition Using* books, the perfect all-in-one resource—and recognized authority on detailed reference information.

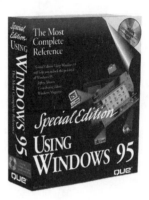

The *Using* series for casual users	*Special Edition Using* for accomplished users
Who should use this book?	**Who should use this book?**

Who should use this book?

Everyday users who:

- Work with computers in the office or at home
- Are familiar with computers but not in love with technology
- Just want to "get the job done"
- Don't want to read a lot of material

Who should use this book?

Proficient computer users who:

- Have a more technical understanding of computers
- Are interested in technological trends
- Want in-depth reference information
- Prefer more detailed explanations and examples

The user-friendly reference

- The fastest access to the one best way to get things done
- Bite-sized information for quick and easy reference
- Nontechnical approach in plain English
- Real-world analogies to explain new concepts
- Troubleshooting tips to help solve problems
- Visual elements and screen pictures that reinforce topics
- Expert authors who are experienced in training and instruction

The most complete reference

- Thorough explanations of various ways to perform tasks
- In-depth coverage of all topics
- Technical information cross-referenced for easy access
- Professional tips, tricks, and shortcuts for experienced users
- Advanced troubleshooting information with alternative approaches
- Visual elements and screen pictures that reinforce topics
- Technically qualified authors who are experts in their fields
- "Techniques form the Pros" sections with advice from well-known computer professionals

Complete and Return this Card
for a *FREE* Computer Book Catalog

Thank you for purchasing this book! You have purchased a superior computer book written expressly for your needs. To continue to provide the kind of up-to-date, pertinent coverage you've come to expect from us, we need to hear from you. Please take a minute to complete and return this self-addressed, postage-paid form. In return, we'll send you a free catalog of all our computer books on topics ranging from word processing to programming and the internet.

Mr. ☐   Mrs. ☐   Ms. ☐   Dr. ☐

Name (first) ☐☐☐☐☐☐☐☐☐☐☐☐   (M.I.) ☐   (last) ☐☐☐☐☐☐☐☐☐☐☐☐☐☐☐☐☐

Address ☐☐☐☐☐☐☐☐☐☐☐☐☐☐☐☐☐☐☐☐☐☐☐☐☐☐☐☐☐☐☐☐

☐☐☐☐☐☐☐☐☐☐☐☐☐☐☐☐☐☐☐☐☐☐☐☐☐☐☐☐☐☐☐☐

City ☐☐☐☐☐☐☐☐☐☐☐☐   State ☐☐   Zip ☐☐☐☐☐ ☐☐☐☐

Phone ☐☐☐ ☐☐☐ ☐☐☐☐   Fax ☐☐☐ ☐☐☐ ☐☐☐☐

Company Name ☐☐☐☐☐☐☐☐☐☐☐☐☐☐☐☐☐☐☐☐☐☐☐☐☐☐☐☐

E-mail address ☐☐☐☐☐☐☐☐☐☐☐☐☐☐☐☐☐☐☐☐☐☐☐☐☐☐☐☐

1. Please check at least (3) influencing factors for purchasing this book.

Front or back cover information on book .... ☐
Special approach to the content .... ☐
Completeness of content .... ☐
Author's reputation .... ☐
Publisher's reputation .... ☐
Book cover design or layout .... ☐
Index or table of contents of book .... ☐
Price of book .... ☐
Special effects, graphics, illustrations .... ☐
Other (Please specify): _____ ☐

2. How did you first learn about this book?

Saw in Macmillan Computer Publishing catalog .... ☐
Recommended by store personnel .... ☐
Saw the book on bookshelf at store .... ☐
Recommended by a friend .... ☐
Received advertisement in the mail .... ☐
Saw an advertisement in: _____ ☐
Read book review in: _____ ☐
Other (Please specify): _____ ☐

3. How many computer books have you purchased in the last six months?

This book only .... ☐   3 to 5 books .... ☐
2 books .... ☐   More than 5 .... ☐

4. Where did you purchase this book?

Bookstore .... ☐
Computer Store .... ☐
Consumer Electronics Store .... ☐
Department Store .... ☐
Office Club .... ☐
Warehouse Club .... ☐
Mail Order .... ☐
Direct from Publisher .... ☐
Internet site .... ☐
Other (Please specify): _____ ☐

5. How long have you been using a computer?

☐ Less than 6 months   ☐ 6 months to a year
☐ 1 to 3 years   ☐ More than 3 years

6. What is your level of experience with personal computers and with the subject of this book?

	With PCs	With subject of book
New	☐	☐
Casual	☐	☐
Accomplished	☐	☐
Expert	☐	☐

Source Code ISBN: 0-7897-0901-5

7. Which of the following best describes your job title?

Administrative Assistant .... ☐
Coordinator .... ☐
Manager/Supervisor .... ☐
Director .... ☐
Vice President .... ☐
President/CEO/COO .... ☐
Lawyer/Doctor/Medical Professional .... ☐
Teacher/Educator/Trainer .... ☐
Engineer/Technician .... ☐
Consultant .... ☐
Not employed/Student/Retired .... ☐
Other (Please specify): _____ ☐

8. Which of the following best describes the area of the company your job title falls under?

Accounting .... ☐
Engineering .... ☐
Manufacturing .... ☐
Operations .... ☐
Marketing .... ☐
Sales .... ☐
Other (Please specify): _____ ☐

9. What is your age?

Under 20 .... ☐
21-29 .... ☐
30-39 .... ☐
40-49 .... ☐
50-59 .... ☐
60-over .... ☐

10. Are you:

Male .... ☐
Female .... ☐

11. Which computer publications do you read regularly? (Please list)

_____
_____
_____
_____
_____
_____
_____
_____
_____
_____

Comments: _____
_____
_____

Fold here and scotch-tape to mail.

Before using any of the software on this disc, you need to install the software you plan to use. See **Appendix D** for directions. If you have problems with the **Creating Your Own AOL Web Pages** CD, please contact Macmillan Technical Support at (317) 581-3833. We can be reached by e-mail at **support@mcp.com** or by CompuServe at **GO QUEBOOKS**.

Read This before Opening Software

By opening this package, you are agreeing to be bound by the following: